One Thousand Words:
A Polyglot's Guide to European Languages

Aanthony A. Aardvark

Rock and Fire Press
2020

One Thousand Words:
A Polyglot's Guide to European Languages
© 2020 by Aanthony A. Aardvark
(a pseudonym)

ISBN 978-1-949005-02-8
(print version)

First Edition, First Printing
August 2020

Rock and Fire Press
Salinas, California

N*I*A*C*IN Denies Any Involvement

One Thousand Words;
The Polyglot's Handbook

Introduction:

This book is wrong. There, I've said it up front, no questions asked. This book is simply wrong. It is wrong in its approach, it is wrong in its data, it is wrong in its format, and it is wrong that a book so wrong can exist. In those few sentences, I have just affirmed everything that a professional linguist will say about this book, or a language teacher, or even most language students.

This book is showing you the wrong approach to language. You are supposed to learn language by one of two methods. The better of the two is throwing yourself headfirst into an environment where only that language is spoken. You must then immerse yourself until you either drown or swim. Alternatively, you must memorize endless conjugations of endless verbs in the most obscure forms and cases, along with whether certain nouns, verbs, and other parts of speech are masculine, feminine, neuter, subjunctive, accusative, interrogatory, or perhaps Methodists. And then you get to work on grammar problems.

Unfortunately, these methods tend to break the student's spirit long before the student has cracked the code. What I hope to do here is to offer a code-book that will allow the student to remain motivated – a book which actually teaches him or her how to say something.

This book is the wrong format for such a book. A book for a student of language is supposed to be a textbook, a dictionary, or a phrasebook. This book is none of those.

It is not a textbook: There are no exercises, no instructions, no table of cases, and no conjugations. There's no pronunciation key. I've even been careless with accent marks.

It is not a dictionary: If you try to look up a specific word, you'll find yourself very frustrated. Mainly because it's not alphabetical.

It is not a phrasebook: You will not find a section "At the Airport," with helpful phrases to say to customs agents, ticket agents, or the pilot of your plane. Okay, I compromised a little bit: On the first page of each language you will find common phrases required for politeness, numbers, and similar important phrases. But that's it.

This book is organized into three columns: An ordinal number, a foreign word, and a brief explanation in English. In that way, it's a bit like a glossary, except that glossaries are usually alphabetical. This book is not. It is instead organized by ordinal numbers. The word next to the number 1 is probably the word you will encounter the most often. The word next to the number 2 is the second most common word, and so forth.

As a point of trivia: The first named word in each section will probably occur once every sixteen words on average. The next word will probably occur one-half as often (1:32) as the first word. The third word will occur about one third as often as the first word. If you're curious how that works, try searching for Zipf's Law.

And that brings me to a third way that this book is wrong: No one really agrees on the frequency of words. Oh, there are lists, and some are generally accurate, but you might find that "And" is fourth on this list, and fifth on that list. To create a truly accurate list requires a sample size that approaches infinity. So if I tell you that "Moazagotl" is the fifty-third word on the list, and the general consensus is that it's actually the seventy-fifth, well, as I said: This book is wrong. So wrong. Oh, just so very wrong.

So, then, what is this book good for? I'm glad that you asked. This book is a kind of a crib sheet for languages. There are about 500,000 words in the English Language, about 300,000 in German, and about 200,000 in French, just to use three examples. But only a small fraction of those words are commonly used. A person who has a working vocabulary of 10,000 words –

that is, if they can correctly use 10,000 English words and understand them well – that person will have an exceptional grasp of the English language. If you have a working everyday English vocabulary that size, you very likely have a college education and are a native speaker of English.

A working vocabulary of 5,000-10,000 words would be enough for most professional editors, writers, and people who work with words on a daily basis. A person with a vocabulary of 3,000 – if they are the right 3,000 words – can probably understand 95% of everything that is written in newspapers, internet blogs, and common sources of written information. In this kind of every-day writing, a mere 1,000 words make up 89% of all writing, and a full third of common everyday writings – store flyers, road signs, and such – use only about the 25 or so most common words.

In addition to words that we understand well, there is a larger cloud of words that we recognize or can figure out easily. Take supernumerary, for example: Well, super is more or bigger, and numerary looks like numeral or number, so supernumerary must mean "A bigger number." Words like that – words we're not closely familiar with, but can recognize and use with reasonable confidence – usually push the average well-educated English-speaker's vocabulary towards the range of 25,000 – 30,000.

But someone who knows only 1,000 English words can function in America. Someone with 3,000 words can pick up any other needed words from contextual clues. And for some languages, those numbers dip even lower.

To make a long story short, the purpose of this book is to kick-start your foreign language learning by giving you about 1,000 words of several languages. 1,000 words, enough for a basic understanding, up front, without the subjunctive plu-perfect in the accusative case where e is preceded by an umlaut.

Armed with that small but powerful vocabulary, it is then your duty to expand it and to learn how to use it. Start reading newspapers or even books in that language. Watch movies with subtitles (preferably movies in the subject language, with subtitles in English). Take courses, or undergo immersion, with confidence, knowing that you have a basic grasp of the most important words, and won't be groping in the dark for a certain key word. Suddenly, learning a language can go from a long, boring, and difficult endeavor, to a task that can be achieved relatively painlessly and efficiently.

It's a matter of stages. The hope is to skip you over the awkward "Where bathroom please please fast?" stage to the "Excuse me, where are the bathrooms?" stage. With luck, perhaps it may even get you towards the "I beg your pardon, Sir, but can you tell me whether the bathrooms on this floor are unisex?" stage.

Will this book make you fluent? No. But it might help you get a head start on fluency.

Will this book make you conversational? Maybe, or perhaps at least give you tools to make yourself conversational more easily.

Now, as I said at the beginning, this book is wrong, and there's another way that it's wrong. It is wrong in the definitions of certain words. This is a necessary evil, given the quick and simple method used here. Definitions give the most important meanings only. If a word has more to it, it's up to you to unpack that further. If I tell you that the English word "Run" means to quickly move yourself to another place using your legs as a means of transportation, then I'm not telling you that it also can mean, "To operate an establishment or business." It's more than I can put in a single line of information.

So read with caution, apply common sense, and use this book as a guide, and not as a manual. Use this book to supplement other learning methods. Or use it as an introduction. With that understood, this should be a very useful and fun book for you. Enjoy it.

But don't sue me if you mistake the Pope (Popa) for a potato (Papa).

SPANISH / ESPAÑOL:

Polite phrases and Important ideas:

Please	Por Favor (poor FAH-vor)
Thanks	Gracias (GRAH-see-us)
Thank you	Gracias
Thank you (emphasis)	Muchos Gracias (MOOch-Ohs GRAH-see-us)

Excuse me (interrupting)	Perdon (PAIR-dohn)
Pardon me (for an error)	Perdon (PAIR-dohn)
Pardon me (for walking in front of someone)	Con Permiso (Kon-PAIR-meeso) ("with permission")
Forgive me (for a grave error)	Disculpe (DIS-cull-pay)
I'm sorry	Lo Siento (LOW SEE-in-toe) (lit. "I feel it")

What is your name?	Como se yama (KOH-Moh say yah-mah?)
My name is…	Yo se yama (YO say Ah-mah) ("I am called…")

Where are the bathrooms?	Donde esta los banos?

1	Uno (OO-no)	6	Seis (SAY-sss)	11	Onse (OHn-say)
2	Dos (DOHss)	7	Siete (SEE-et-tay)	12	Dose (DOH-say)
3	Tres (TRAYss)	8	Ocho (OH-cho)	13	Trese (TRAY-say)
4	Quatro (KWAH-troh)	9	Nueve (NU-ev-AY)	14	Quatoze (KAT-OH-say)
5	Cinco (SINK-oh)	10	Diez (DEE-az)	15	Quince (KEEN-say)

16	Dieciséis, (Dee-SAY-ss)	21	Venta-uno	70	Setenta
17	Diecisiete (Dee-See-Ett-Ay)	30	Triente	80	Ochenta
18	Dieciocho (Dee-See-OhCho)	40	Cuarenta	90	Noventa
19	Diecinueve(Dee-see-noo-efay)	50	Cincuenta	100	Ceinte (SEEIN-tay)
20	Venta (VINN-tah)	60	Sesenta	1000	Mille (MEE-luh)

10,000 Diez Mille		1,000,000 Un Millon	0 Cero

Odd Cases and Special Phrases:

Besame – *Kiss me.*	(BASSuh-may)
Pasale – *Pass it.*	(PASSuh-lay) (a common response to "Con Permiso")
Ondele – *Hurry it (up).*	(ON-delay) (slightly aggressive) also ORA-lay (very aggressive)
No se – *Don't Know*	(Noh-Say) (implied "I")
Calmate – *Calm yourself*	(CAHL-ma-tay)
Vente – *Come on!*	(VINN-tay) (as a parent to a dawdling child)
No me gusto – *I don't like (it)*	(Noh-MEE-goose-toe) ("It doesn't please me")
No comprendo – *(I) Don't understand*	(Noh-COM-PREN-doe)

In SPANISH, a familiar noun may be attached to the end of a verb, creating a command such as besame, pasale, ondele, calmate, or vente. There are also "Spanglish" words like "Watch-a-le!" (Watch it!) (Look out!)

Top 1000 words:

1	el / la	the
2	y	and
3	de	of or from
4	qué	than, what, or that
5	no	not or no, general negation
6	a	to
7	es	is (See *estar*)
8	en	in, into
9	se	himself / herself
10	lo	it, *lo siento*, [I] feel it (I'm sorry)
11	haber	to have, see *hay, había*
12	un, uno, una	a, an, one
13	por	for, by, (*por favor*, please)
14	te	you, personal and intimate: *Te ama, mi amor!*
15	se	is
16	su	his, hers, theirs
17	los (m, plural)	the
18	con	with
19	para	for, or in order to
20	si	if, yes, whether
21	pero	but (do not confuse with *perro*, dog)
22	las (f, plural)	the
23	bien	nice, well, fine, good, (*Bienestar*, Good health)
24	yo	I (see also *mi, me*)
25	su	your or their (*Mi casa es su casa*, My house is your home)
26	eso	that
27	más	more or another
28	aquí	here
29	del(m), de la (f)	of the
30	o	or
31	al	to the … or at the …
32	poder	to be able to
33	cómo	like, how or as (*Como yo soy*, Just as I am)
34	le	him or it (*Pasa le*, pass it)
35	ir	to go
36	esto, este	this, this one
37	vamos	let's go, lit. "we go," cf. *Vamanos*, "we're going!"
38	ahora	now
39	la	it (feminine)
40	hay	there are …
41	estoy	I am (see *estar*)
42	me	me (*¿Cuándo me va a llamar?* When will you call me?)
43	algo	something, anything
44	ya	already, still
45	tú, ti	You, in a personal sense, as to a lover or close friend
46	ver	to see
47	tengo	I have (see *haber*)
48	así	so, thus, like that, (asi asi, kind of, so-so)
49	nada	nothing (yo no se nada, I know nothing about that)

50	nos	us
51	cuando	when, whenever, (do not confuse with *Quanto*, how much)
52	muy	very
53	él	he
54	sin	without
55	sé	know
56	estás	these
57	saber	to know
58	sólo	only or alone, just (as merely), see *Soledad, Solomiente*
59	quiero, quieres	to want (from verb *querer*)
60	sobre	about
61	tiene, tienes	you have (from verb *tiener*)
62	alguno	some
63	gracias	thank you, *muchos gracias*, thank you very much
64	he	have
65	soy	am; *como yo soy*, [just] as I am
66	ser	to be (from verb *estar*)
67	vez	time as repetition, this time, another time, last time
68	hacer	to do or to make
69	todos, todo, toda	every, all
70	ella	she, her
71	querer	to want
72	son	their
73	eres	you are (from verb *estar*),
74	primero, primera	first
75	desde	since
76	usted	you (use this form of you with strangers)
77	señor,	sir, lord, mister (contextual), *El Senor*, The Lord (God)
78	ese	that, alt. Spanglish: buddy
79	voy	goes, went
80	quién	who or whom (*quién habla?* Who speaks?)
81	casa	house; *va a la casa*, go home; *a mi casa*, my place
82	creo	Believe, trust, have faith
83	porque	because, *porque?* why?
84	favor	favor, favorite; *por favor*, please (lit. "as a favor to me")
85	hola	Hi there, Hello
86	día	the day
87	dónde	where; *A donde?*, where to?
88	nunca	never or ever (depending on context)
89	sus (plural)	their
90	sabes	knows (from *saber*, to know) (do not confuse *sabor*, flavor)
91	deber	should
92	dos	two
93	verdad	truth, *es verdad?*, Is it true? Really?
94	angeles	angels
95	poner	to put
96	cosa	thing
97	mucho	much, compare *muy*, many
98	entonces	then (in time, as this then that)
99	tanto	so much
100	parecer	to appear

101	tiempo	time as clock time, see *vez / veces* for repetitions
102	mí	me (as object), *par mi*, for me
103	nuestro	our
104	mejor	better; *el mejor*, the best
105	tan	so much
106	hombre	man, compare *Cabellero*, man
107	va	go
108	Dios	God; *adios*, to God (I entrust you), *Vaya con Dios*, go with God
109	también	as well, also
110	vida, vido	life; *vida loca*, crazy life
111	quedar	to stay
112	siempre	always; *siempre mucho*, more of the same
113	creer	to believe
114	hasta	until, *Hasta luego*, until later
115	ahí	over there
116	llevar	to wear, carry
117	siento	to feel, *Lo Siento,* I'm sorry (lit. I feel it)
118	decir	to say, decide
119	dejar	to leave
120	ni	neither, nor (*ni este ni esta mi gusto,* neither this nor that pleases me)
121	seguir	to follow
122	tenemos	we have
123	menos	less, fewer or minus
124	cosas	stuff, things, lit. "causes;" *no esta una cosa grande,* it's no big deal
125	ante, antes	before
126	mi, mis	my
127	poco	little, a few, short
128	pues	then, well then
129	llamar	to call, *Gracias para llamada,* thank you for having called.
130	otra, otro	other
131	padre	father or parent, see also *madre*, mother
132	venir	to come
133	gente	people as a crowd, compare *pueblo*, people as a community
134	pensar	to think
135	aquel	that (over there)
136	parece	to seem or to appear
137	dinero	money, see also *precio*, price, *precioso*, expensive or costly
138	estar	to be
139	sino	but rather, instead
140	hecho	made (from *hacir*, to make)
141	mismo	the same as
142	mira	look, sometimes an interjection: *Mira, yo no se,* Look, I don't know
143	pasa, paso	pass, passage
144	trabajo	work; *trabajando*, working, *trabajadore/ trabajadora*, worker
145	claro	clear, fig. I understand; naturally, clearly, OK
146	mañana	morning, tomorrow
147	después	after or later
148	mundo	world, everything
149	tres	very, compare *muchos* and *muy*
150	hablar	to speak
151	tal	such

152	había	to have
153	acuerdo	agreement or deal, accord, OK then
154	cierto	true, certain, absolutely
155	conocer	to meet, know
156	momento	moment as time; *uno momento por favor*, one moment, please
157	hacía	toward, towards
158	hijo	son, compare *mijo*, my son, *muchacho*, dear boy, *nino*, boy
159	podría	could (has the power to)
160	seguro	safe, secure, reliable *seguridad* Safety
161	mujer	woman
162	amigo	friend
163	madre	mother, compare *padre*, father or parent
164	sentir	to feel, *lo siento*, I feel it, I sympathize
165	luego	later *Hasta Luego,* until later (greeting when parting)
166	sympatico	friendly, gracious, sympathetic
167	país	country
168	tus	your (personal, as to a close friend)
169	lugar	location, place, compare *plaza,* place
170	tratar	to try
171	especial	special
172	gusta, gusto	to please, pleasing, pleasant, pleasure, *mi gusto,* it pleases me, I like it.
173	persona	person
174	será	it is, from the verb *estar,* to be
175	grande, gran	large or huge
176	mayor	larger, older, main
177	espera	to wait
178	último	last, final
179	hoy	today
180	propio	own, *pro propio,* for oneself.
181	tener	to have, *tiens usted?* do you have (it)?
182	mirar	to look, to watch
183	estado	state, condition, status
184	ninguno	none, nobody
185	tres	three, not to beconfused with *tres,* very
186	debe	should
187	punto	point, dot, period, also point as peninsula
188	verdugo	vegetable
189	mal, malo	bad, pain, disease; *tengo malo a mi cabeza,* my head hurts
190	nombre	name
191	fecha	date
192	crees	create
193	manera	way, manner
194	cual	which, who, whom
195	firma	signature
196	amor	to love, *ama* I love, *amo* you/he/she love(s)
197	familia	family
198	mientras	meanwhile, while, whereas, as long as
199	realidad	reality, actuality
200	contar	to count, to tell
201	entender	to understand, to listen
202	mío	mine,

203	pedir	to ask for, request
204	fin	end
205	recibir	to receive
206	obra	work, book, deed
207	visto	viewed
208	importante	important
209	medio	medium, half, middle
210	tipo	type, kind
211	fruta	fruit,
212	además	in addition to, also, as well, besides
213	mes	month
214	contigo	with, alongside, beside
215	todavía	still, yet
216	caja	box,
217	empezar	to begin
218	bajo	under, underneath
219	importa	importance
220	ejemplo	example (*por ejemplo*, for example)
221	recordar	to remember, remind
222	grupo	group
223	parte	part
224	familiar	familiar, of the family
225	esperar	to wait
226	mil, mille	thousand
227	humano	human
228	nuestra, nuestro	our,
229	cada	each
230	terminar	to finish, end
231	hora	hour
232	permitir	to allow, permit
233	aparecer	to appear
234	necesitar	to need, *necesita*, I need, *necesito*, you need, *necesario*, necessary
235	allí	there
236	conseguir	to get, acquire, obtain
237	comenzar	to begin, start
238	fatigado	exhausted
239	ayuda	help; *Ayudame! (Iy-Ooo-DAH-MAY!)* Help me!
240	varios	several, various
241	posible	possible
242	problema	problem
243	buenas (f)	good
244	servir	to serve
245	general	general
246	hacerlo	do this, do it
247	contra	against, opposite, opposing,
248	sacar	to take out
249	dicho	said, *el dicho, la dicha,* he said, she said.
250	necesitar	to need
251	buscar	to look for
252	relación	relationship, relation
253	cinco	five

254	demasiado	too much, too many
255	cuerpo	body, see also *mente*, mind
256	dentro	within, inside
257	nadie	nobody, anybody
258	oye	hear
259	largo	long, large
260	mantener	to keep, maintain
261	entre	between
262	hecho, hecha	manufactured, made
263	ante	before, in the presence of
264	palabra	word
265	adiós	goodbye
266	principio	beginning, principle
267	existir	to exist
268	resultar	to result, turn out
269	igual	equal, same (as)
270	niño	child, especially a boy
271	entrar	to enter
272	ojos	eyes
273	embargo	barrier, *sin embargo*, however, nevertheless
274	tarde	afternoon, evening
275	segundo	second
276	vaya	go
277	leer	to read
278	único	only, unique, sole
279	caer	to fall
280	razón	reason,
281	alguna	any
282	cambiar	to change
283	ojo	eye
284	trabajar	to work
285	calle	street
286	confundido	confused
287	presentar	to introduce, to present
288	sangre	blood
289	blanco	white
290	cambio	change
291	crear	to create
292	escribir	to write
293	abrir	to open
294	pues	could or could be
295	cuatro	four
296	libro	book
297	distinto	distinct, different
298	veo	see
299	chica	girl
300	fuerza	strength, force, power
301	luz	light
302	perder	to lose
303	según	according to
304	nosotro	we

305	santo	saint (m)
306	policía	police
307	cabeza	head (of a person or animal)
308	frente	front, *al frente*: facing, *frente a*: across from
309	considerar	to consider
310	idea	idea
311	ustedes	you, plural
312	agua	water
313	oír	to hear
314	cuyo	whose
315	sazon	spice, seasoning
316	hermano	brother, compare *hermana*, sister, *'mano-a-'mano*, as brothers
317	sentido	sense, feeling
318	acabar	finish
319	producir	to produce
320	noche	night
321	pasó	passage
322	serio	serious,
323	situación	situation
324	cuidad	city
325	bastante	rather, fairly, quite a bit
326	modo	way, manner
327	convertir	to convert, change, become
328	muerto	dead
329	gracia	thank you; grace, favor
330	ocurrir	to occur
331	siglo	century, age
332	dios	god, divinity
333	salir	to depart, to leave a place, *salida*, exit
334	pasado	passed, as to have been passed by
335	cuenta	count
336	tierra	earth, land, ground
337	cariño, carina	beloved, dear friend, dear one
338	papel	paper, documents
339	treinta	thirty
340	televisión	TV, television
341	vale	voucher
342	señora	Mrs. or lady
343	tampoco	neither, nor, either
344	social	social
345	rápido	fast,
346	viejo	old
347	lado	side
348	tema	theme, subject, topic
349	debería	should
350	político	political
351	cuidado	attention
352	español	Spanish
353	buenos	good
354	ganar	to win, earn
355	formar	to form

356	pongo	to put or to place
357	sería	will
358	enojado	angry
359	traer	to bring, carry
360	mientras	while
361	partir	to divide, leave; *a partir de:* starting, from the start
362	miedo	fear
363	prima, primo	first quality, first rank
364	morir	to die
365	puerta	door
366	casi	almost
367	incluso	including, even
368	campo	field, country
369	nueva, nuevo	new
370	aceptar	to accept
371	furioso	enraged, furious, livid
372	espero	I hope
373	quizás, quiza	perhaps, maybe
374	cerebro	brain
375	cualquier	however
376	deprimido	depressed
377	realizar	to fulfill, carry out
378	ciento	hundred
379	playa	beach
380	laguna	lagoon
381	chico	boy, see *chica*, girl, *niño, niña*
382	cuánto	how much
383	niños	children, boys or mixed gender; see *niñas*, girls
384	camino	way, road, highway
385	piensé	think
386	lastimado	hurt, injured
387	debes	you must
388	leal	loyal
389	historia	history, tale, story, recounting
390	año	year, note that ñ is important
391	deja	allow
392	durante	during, while
393	forma	form
394	cama	bed
395	volver	turn, return, come back
396	feliz	happy, fortunate
397	guerra	war; *guerilla,* little war
398	caso	case
399	esposa	wife
400	mano	hand, do not confuse with *'mano*, short for *hermano*
401	hice	to do
402	gustaría	would like, would be pleased by
403	loco	crazy
404	minutos	minute as a unit of time
405	entiendo	understand
406	toma	to drink, to take (medicine)

407	pasar	to pass by
408	jefe	leader, boss, manager, supervisor
409	corazón	heart, *estoi loco in mi corazon par ti*, I am crazy in my heart for you
410	semana	week
411	juntos, junta	together, group, team
412	supongo	suppose
413	tarde	late
414	déjame	let me (go), allow me
415	lista	list, roster, roll, do not confuse *listo*, ready
416	vete	yourself
417	niña	child, young girl
418	personas	people
419	hablando	talking,
420	cara	face
421	ningún	any,
422	bajo/baja	low, *Baja California*, Lower California (a peninsula in Mexico)
423	escucha	listening
424	tío	uncle, *tia*, aunt
425	aunque	although
426	guyena	hen
427	siquiera	even
428	gaviota	seagull
429	cerca	near
430	pequeño	small, a little bit, *yo habla pequeño de Español*, I speak a little Spanish
431	dame	give
432	sigue	follow
433	auto	car
434	aguila	eagle
435	fuego	fire
436	listo	ready, do not confuse *lista,* list
437	significa	to mean, to signify
438	capitán	captain, leader, foreman
439	clase	class
440	suspechoso	suspicious
441	llegar	to arrive
442	tomar	to drink, or to take (medicine, pills)
443	vivir	to live
444	joven	young person
445	abajo	below
446	lugar	place, location, spot
447	genial	brilliant
448	justo	right, in the moral sense; just
449	comer	to eat
450	conozco	know
451	fuerte	strong
452	número	number
453	gavilan	hawk
454	basta	Enough!
455	dar	give
456	dueño, duena	owner, landlord
457	atrás	in back of, behind

458	éste	this
459	pueda, puede	to be able
460	vino	wine
461	escuela	school
462	podía	he could
463	pueblo	people, as a group or community, *mi pueblo*, my people
464	meses	months
465	coche	car (automobile or train)
466	juego	game, play, sport, *juego el juego con me*, play the game with me.
467	encontrar	to find
468	esperanza/esperanzo	to hope, to wait
469	última	last, final, ultimate
470	paz	peace
471	dime	tell me, say to me
472	vuelta	turn, *revuelta*, return, go back
473	tenido	had
474	ido	gone
475	querida	mistress
476	culpa	fault
477	dólares	dollars
478	escrito	marked, written
479	fácil	easy
480	alto	high
481	posible	possible
482	dormir	to sleep
483	pregunta	question
484	fiesta	party, feast, festival
485	lejos	away
486	preocupes	concerns, distractions, problems, burdens
487	soledad	lonely, alone, only
488	bomba	pump, *bombadero*, fireman
489	niñas	girls
490	ventana	window
491	solomiente	only, solely
492	leche	milk
493	peligro	danger, *peligroso/peligrosa* dangerous
494	dereche, derecha	right (as "right hand," *mano dereche*)
495	serioso	serious
496	bombadero	fireman
497	orden	order
498	mover	to move, incite
499	continuar	to continue
500	cantidad	quantity, amount
501	acción	action, act, deed
502	suceder	to happen
503	fijar	to set, fix, *se fijar*, to notice or realize
504	sociedad	society
505	referir	to refer (to)
506	acercar	to come near
507	capaz	capable, able
508	ordernar	one who makes orders, marshal, Captain

509	libre	free, vacant
510	natural	natural
511	dedicar	to dedicate, devote
512	grado	degree, grade
513	realmente	really, actually, in fact
514	peso	peso (money), weight, load, *pesado,* heavy
515	efecto	effect
516	objeto	object, thing
517	verdadero	true, real
518	dónde	where?
519	aprender	to learn
520	amor	love
521	partido	match (sports)
522	económico	economic
523	derecho	right, justice, law
524	poderoso	powerful
525	importancia	importance
526	sistema	system
527	viaje	travel, trip
528	suelo	ground, floor
529	respeto	respect, *con respeto a*: with regards to
530	conocimiento	knowledge, science
531	libertad	freedom, liberty
532	encima	above, on top, in addition
533	comprar	to buy
534	común	common
535	abierto	open, unlocked
536	próximo	next
537	atención	attention
538	subir	to go up
539	esfuerzo	effort, endeavor
540	tirer	to dispose, to throw, to throw away, to discard
541	evitar	to avoid, prevent
542	resto	rest, remainder, leftover
543	interesar	to interest
544	zona	area, zone
545	sabor	flavor
546	fuera	out, outside, away
547	proceso	process, procedure
548	vivo	alive, bright
549	cerrar	to close
550	echar	to throw, cast
551	responder	to answer, respond
552	sufrir	to suffer, undergo
553	completo	complete
554	picante	spicy
555	contrario	contrary, opposite
556	mesa	table, board
557	real	royal, real, authentic
558	ocasión	opportunity, occasion
559	personaje	character (e.g. movie)

560	importar	to matter, import
561	público	public, audience
562	obtener	to obtain
563	programa	program, plan
564	siete	seven
565	enorme	enormous, vast
566	respuesta	answer, reply
567	línea	line, course
568	espacio	space, room
569	nivel	level
570	gobierno	government
571	cabo	end, bit; *llevar a cabo*, to bring to its conclusion, to complete
572	observar	to observe
573	indicar	to indicate
574	alguien	somebody, someone, anyone
575	imagen	image, picture
576	carrera	career, course, race
577	imaginar	to imagine
578	soler	to do as a habit, to be accustomed to do
579	ambos	both
580	profundo	deep, profound
581	detener	to stop, detain
582	desarrollar	to develop
583	ocho	eight
584	señalar	to point (out), signal
585	elegir	to choose, elect
586	figura	figure
587	principal	main, principal
588	animal	animal
589	base	base, basis
590	duro	hard
591	preparar	to prepare
592	proponer	to propose
593	don	courtesy title (m), Mr., gift
594	suponer	to suppose, assume
595	comprender	to understand
596	final	final
597	interés	interest
598	siguiente	following, next
599	vista	view, sight
600	lograr	to achieve, get, manage
601	demás	the rest, others
602	difícil	difficult, hard
603	explicar	to explain
604	negro	black
605	fondo	bottom, end
606	voz	voice
607	estudio	study, learning
608	necesario	necessary
609	preguntar	to ask (a question)
610	allá	there, over there

611	tocar	to touch, play (instrument)
612	valor	value, worth
613	reconocer	to recognize, admit
614	estudiar	to study
615	alcanzar	to reach, catch up with
616	nacer	to be born
617	dirigir	to direct, manage
618	correr	to run
619	medida	measure; *a medida que*: to the extent that
620	menor	younger, youngest
621	solamente	only
622	bueno	well or good
623	utilizar	to use, utilize
624	centro	center, middle, downtown
625	necesidad	necessity, need *necessita*, I need, *necessito*, you need
626	condición	condition
627	pagar	to pay
628	ello	it
629	falta	lack, shortage, fault
630	ayudar	to help
631	diez	ten
632	comparar	to compare
633	través	traverse, *a través*, across, over, through
634	antiguo	old, ancient, former
635	edad	age
636	gustar	to be pleasing to
637	jugar	to play (sport/game)
638	mí	me (obj prep)
639	época	time, age, period
640	color	color
641	escuchar	to listen to
642	experiencia	experience
643	movimiento	movement
644	cumplirto	fulfill
645	diferente	different, separate
646	pesar	sorrow, weight, or burden; *a pesar de*: in spite of
647	posibilidad	possibility
648	ofrecer	to offer, present
649	descubrir	to discover
650	anterior	previous, preceding
651	levantar	to raise, lift
652	pobre	poor
653	aire	air, wind, appearance
654	seis	six
655	intentarto	try, attempt
656	saboroso	flavorful
657	junto, junta	together with, next to
658	resultado	result, outcome
659	usar	to use
660	decidir	to decide
661	repetir	to repeat

662	olvidar	to forget
663	ley	law, bill, rule
664	aspecto	aspect, appearance
665	pie	foot, base
666	valer	to be worth, cost
667	especie	kind, sort, species
668	servicio	service, helpfulness
669	mostrar	to show
670	actividad	activity, action
671	tercero	third
672	cuál	which?
673	pronto	soon, quick
674	ocupar	to occupy, use
675	cuestión	question (subject) under discussion, matter, topic
676	duda	doubt
677	diferencia	difference
678	demostrar	to show, demonstrate
679	significar	to mean, to signify
680	posición	position
681	motivo	motive, cause
682	prueba	proof, trial, test
683	política	politics, policy
684	nacional	national
685	lleno	full, filled
686	reunir	to gather, meet, collect
687	faltar	to be lacking, to be faulty
688	supuesto	supposed; *por supuesto*: of course
689	acompañar	to accompany
690	dato	data, fact
691	desear	to want, desire, wish for
692	mitad	half, middle
693	adelante	forward, further
694	empresa	firm, company, venture
695	asunto	matter, issue, affair
696	celebrar	to celebrate
697	presencia	presence, appearance
698	suyo	his, hers, yours (-fam), theirs
699	cultura	culture
700	serie	series
701	millón	million, fortune
702	enseñarto	teach, show
703	construir	to construct, build
704	vender	to sell
705	representar	to represent
706	desaparecer	to disappear, vanish
707	mandar	to send, order
708	carácter	personality, nature
709	mayoría	majority
710	escuela	school
711	rojo	red
712	tras	after, behind

713	superior	superior, upper
714	andar	to walk, function
715	corto	short, brief
716	batalla	battle
717	autor	writer, author
718	conocido	known, well-known
719	preferir	to prefer
720	asegurar	to assure, secure, insure
721	función	function, meeting
722	arriba	up above
723	causa	cause
724	suficiente	sufficient, enough, adequate
725	grave	serious, solemn
726	decisión	decision
727	música	music
728	extraño	strange, foreign
729	crecer	to grow, increase
730	surgir	to appear, spring (forth)
731	expresión	expression
732	alrededor	about, around, round
733	capital	capital; city (f), money (m)
734	matar	to kill
735	entregar	to deliver
736	río	river
737	seguridad	security, safety
738	término	term (language), end
739	colocar	to place, position
740	metro	meter, subway
741	médico	doctor
742	establecer	to establish
743	guardar	to keep, save
744	arte	art, skill
745	iniciar	to initiate, start
746	bajar	to come down, let down
747	consecuencia	consequence
748	notar	to notice
749	acto	act, action
750	meter	to put (into)
751	absoluto	absolute
752	pena	trouble; *valer la pena*: worth the trouble
753	actuar	to act
754	altura	height, altitude
755	deseo	desire, wish
756	precisamente	precisely
757	joven	teenager, young person
758	veinte	twenty
759	sueño	dream, sleep
760	pretender	to attempt
761	tarea	task, job
762	carta	letter, (playing) card
763	apenas	hardly, barely

764	propiedad	property
765	producto	product
766	personal	personal
767	simplemente	simply, just
768	imposible	impossible
769	gusto, gusta	pleasure, taste, preference
770	acordar	to remember, remind
771	lengua	language, tongue, strip (of land), peninsula
772	cortar	to cut
773	plan	plan
774	corresponder	to correspond with
775	romper	to break
776	siquiera	even (if)
777	adquirir	to acquire, get
778	proyecto	project, plan
779	memoria	memory
780	origen	origin, cause
781	elemento	element
782	inglés	English
783	mercado	market
784	curso	course, direction
785	recurso	resource, recourse, means
786	tirar	to throw, pull
787	lanzar	to throw, launch
788	aprovechar	to take advantage of
789	interior	interior, inside
790	apoyar	to support, lean on
791	negar	to deny, refuse
792	avanzar	to advance, progress
793	uso	use
794	brazo	arm
795	profesor	professor, teacher
796	resolver	to resolve, settle, work out
797	futuro	future
798	oportunidad	opportunity, chance
799	costar	to cost, be hard
800	rico	rich, tasty
801	recuerdo	memory, keepsake
802	total	total, entire
803	exigir	to demand
804	opinión	opinion, view
805	aumentar	to increase
806	recoger	to pick up
807	boca	mouth, entrance, opening
808	dirección	direction, address
809	puro	pure, clean
810	abandonar	to abandon, leave (a place)
811	pieza	piece, part
812	profesional	professional
813	imponer	to impose, enforce
814	obligar	to obligate, force

815	físico	physical
816	merecer	to deserve, be worthy (of)
817	actitud	attitude
818	mar	sea
819	francés	French
820	entrada	entrance, admission ticket
821	contacto	contact
822	aplicar	to apply
823	rápido	quick, fast
824	título	title, heading
825	pertenecer	to belong (to), to pertain (to)
826	cuarto	room, chamber
827	material	material, element
828	golpe	hit, strike, punch
829	disponer	to have means, dispose
830	comunicación	communication
831	expresar	to express
832	simple	simple, mere, simple-minded
833	totalmente	totally, completely
834	provocar	to cause, provoke
835	normal	normal, usual, regular
836	defender	to defend, protect
837	enfermedad	illness, sickness
838	bien	goods, property, benefit
839	materia	matter, subject
840	quitar	to remove, take away
841	conservar	to conserve, preserve
842	moderno	modern
843	sitio	place, space
844	depender	to depend on
845	naturaleza	nature, character
846	capacidad	capacity
847	actual	current
848	marcar	to mark, note, dial
849	distancia	distance
850	pleno	complete, full
851	cerrado	closed
852	compartir	to share
853	información	information
854	ambiente	environment, atmosphere
855	especialmente	especially
856	desarrollo	development
857	sol	sun
858	consistir	to consist of
859	constituir	to constitute, consist of
860	dispuesto	willing, ready
861	cubrir	to cover
862	funcionar	to work, function
863	compañero	companion, classmate
864	salida	exit, escape, outcome
865	caber	to fit (into)

866	conciencia	conscience, consciousness
867	atender	to serve, attend to
868	enfermo	ill, sick
869	insistir	to insist on
870	costumbre	habit, custom, usage
871	detrás	behind
872	noticia	news
873	circunstancia	circumstance
874	dolor	pain, ache, sorrow
875	privado	private
876	estilo	style
877	precio	price, cost, value, *precioso*, dear, valued, expensive
878	popular	popular
879	sentar	to sit (down), seat
880	planta	plant, floor
881	famoso	famous, well-known
882	éxito	success
883	hija	daughter
884	edificio	building
885	autoridad	authority
886	piedra	stone, rock
887	incluir	to include
888	conjunto	group, set, things placed together
889	inmediato	immediate
890	suerte	luck, fortune
891	cruzar	to cross
892	tender	to tend to, lay out
893	civil	civil
894	finalmente	finally, at last
895	anunciar	to announce, advertise
896	espíritu	spirit, ghost
897	miembro	member, limb
898	directo	direct, straight
899	despertar	to wake (up), arouse
900	pared	(interior) wall
901	equipo	team, equipment, outfit
902	error	error, mistake
903	preciso	precise, necessary
904	diverso	different, several, diverse
905	saltar	to jump, leap, hop
906	dificultad	difficulty, obstacle
907	comentar	to comment on
908	incorporar	to incorporate, include
909	publicar	to publish
910	voluntad	will, willpower, intention
911	reunión	meeting, reunion
912	modelo	model, pattern
913	cargar	to load (up), carry, charge (as a battery)
914	participar	to participate
915	impedirto	prevent, hinder
916	propósito	intention, purpose

917	salvar	to save, rescue, *salvador*, savior
918	puesto	job, place, position
919	escapar	to escape
920	lucha	fight, struggle, wrestle
921	entero	entire, whole, complete
922	interesante	interesting
923	amplio	wide, ample, broad
924	contestar	to answer, reply
925	periódico	newspaper, periodical
926	preocupar	to worry
927	prestar	to lend
928	par	pair, couple (m); *a la par*: at same time
929	calidad	quality
930	exponer	to expound, expose
931	ciencia	science, knowledge
932	numeroso	numerous
933	tamaño	size, dimension
934	doctor	doctor
935	cuadro	painting, picture
936	caballo	horse
937	responsabilidad	responsibility
938	cincuenta	fifty
939	interno	internal
940	detalle	detail
941	marcha	march, progress
942	nueve	nine
943	carne	meat, flesh
944	jamás	never
945	pensamiento	thought, thinking
946	viajar	to travel
947	cargo	position, charge, fee
948	separar	to separate
949	santa	saint (f)
950	construcción	construction
951	juicio	judgment
952	terreno	ground, earth, terrain
953	piso	floor, story
954	compañía	company
955	regresar	to return (to a place), regress
956	texto	text
957	fuente	source; fountain
958	definitivo	definitive, conclusive
959	revista	magazine, journal
960	máquina	machine
961	contemplar	to contemplate
962	recorrer	to travel, cover (distance)
963	frase	phrase
964	perfecto	perfect
965	sala	room, hall, see *quarto*, room or chamber
966	durar	to last
967	instrumento	instrument

968	aquello	over there (n)
969	defensa	defense, plea, apology
970	director	director, manager, principal
971	retirar	to take away, retire
972	explicación	explanation
973	artículo	article, product, item
974	debajo	underneath, below
975	permanecer	to stay, remain
976	asistir	to attend
977	doce	twelve
978	radio	radio
979	organizar	to organize
980	película	movie, film
981	elección	election, choice
982	visita	visit, visitor, guest
983	contener	to contain
984	apoyo	support, backing
985	presidente	president
986	arma	weapon
987	árbol	tree
988	pintura	painting, paint
989	visitar	to visit
990	informar	to inform
991	encuentro	meeting, game, skirmish
992	parecido	similar
993	corriente	current, flow, *al corriente*, up to date
994	lectura	reading
995	oficial	official, authorized
996	existencia	existence, life, being
997	lenguaje	language, speech
998	enviar	to send
999	aun	even (though), still
1000	destino	destination, destiny
1001	educación	education
1002	cuidar	to take care of
1003	intervenir	to intervene
1004	operación	operation
1005	raro	strange, rare, scarce
1006	perfectamente	perfectly
1007	extender	to extend, spread
1008	comprobar	to verify, prove
1009	nota	note, grade
1010	particular	particular, peculiar
1011	ése	that one (m), [ésa (f)]
1012	militar	military
1013	dormir	to sleep
1014	unido	united
1015	discutir	to argue, discuss
1016	extraordinario	extraordinary, exceptional
1017	teatro	theater, drama
1018	enfrentar	to confront, face

1019	recién	recently, just
1020	negocio	business, transaction
1021	letra	letter, handwriting, lyrics
1022	peor	worse
1023	sentimiento	feeling, sentiment
1024	conducir	to lead, drive
1025	completamente	completely
1026	firmar	to sign
1027	solución	solution, answer
1028	mío	mine
1029	comida	food, meal
1030	impresión	impression, printing
1031	plano	plane, map, level
1032	intención	intention
1033	ritmo	rhythm
1034	verde	green
1035	exacto	exact, faithful, true
1036	respetar	to respect
1037	banco	(financial) bank, bench
1038	inmediatamente	immediately
1039	sostener	to support, hold up, sustain
1040	piel	skin, hide, fur
1041	delante	(in) front (of), ahead
1042	religioso	religious
1043	advertirto	notice, warn
1044	oscuro	dark, obscure
1045	control	control
1046	investigación	investigation
1047	transformar	to transform, change
1048	conversación	conversation
1049	verano	summer
1050	respeto	respect, regard
1051	norte	north
1052	mediante	by means of
1053	cuarto	fourth
1054	tradición	tradition
1055	bastar	to be sufficient
1056	población	population
1057	pareja	couple, pair
1058	basura	trash, refuse
1059	diario	newspaper
1060	azúl	blue
1061	mencionar	to mention, cite
1062	generación	generation
1063	frío	cold
1064	visión	vision
1065	concreto	concrete, real
1066	plantear	to propose, present
1067	probar	to test, prove, try, probe
1068	derecho	right, straight
1069	oro	gold

1070	manejar	to drive, handle, control, manage
1071	unir	to unite, join (together)
1072	caminar	to walk
1073	coincidir	to coincide, agree
1074	etapa	stage, period, step
1075	sencillo	simple, plain, easy
1076	silencio	silence
1077	salvo	save, except (for), but
1078	llenar	to fill
1079	accidente	accident, irregularity
1080	dominar	to dominate, master
1081	determinado	determined, fixed
1082	artista	artist, performer
1083	medir	to measure
1084	labor	labor, work, task
1085	perdido	lost, compare *perdo*, lost
1086	cielo	sky, heaven, ceiling
1087	práctica	practice, skill
1088	límite	limit
1089	masa	mass, also corn meal
1090	directamente	directly, straight away
1091	atravesar	to cross
1092	formación	formation, education
1093	perro	dog
1094	izquierda	left
1095	destacar	to emphasize, stand out
1096	cercano	near
1097	cuarenta	forty
1098	pronunciar	to pronounce
1099	distinguir	to distinguish
1100	caballo	horse
1101	confianza	confidence, trust
1102	adecuado	adequate, suitable
1103	introducir	to introduce, bring in
1104	flor	flower
1105	comunicar	to communicate
1106	italiano	Italian
1107	invitar	to invite
1108	responsible	responsible
1109	revolución	revolution
1110	instalar	to install
1111	tardar	to delay, take long
1112	mejorar	to improve, get better
1113	maestro	teacher (m), master
1114	emplear	to employ
1115	alemán	German
1116	convenir	to be agreeable, be convenient
1117	recuperar	to recuperate, recover
1118	fenómeno	phenomenon
1119	fundamental	fundamental
1120	presión	pressure

1121	dado	given
1122	alumno	student, pupil
1123	teoría	theory
1124	probablemente	probably
1125	tono	tone
1126	referencia	reference, allusion
1127	salud	health
1128	definir	to define
1129	superar	to overcome, surpass
1130	exactamente	exactly
1131	afirmar	to assert, affirm
1132	histórico	historical
1133	debido, debido a	due to
1134	vía, por vía	by means; road, way
1135	interpretar	to interpret
1136	alma	soul
1137	admitir	to admit
1138	identificar	to identify
1139	madera	wood
1140	calor	heat, warmth
1141	mínimo	minimum
1142	afectar	to affect
1143	hogar	home, hearth
1144	mente	mind
1145	seguramente	surely, securely
1146	preocupación	worry, concern
1147	reducir	to reduce
1148	concepto	concept
1149	montar	to ride, mount, assemble
1150	teléfono	phone, telephone
1151	hoja	sheet, leaf
1152	parar	to stop, cease, come to a halt
1153	doble	double
1154	devolver	to return, give back
1155	ejercer	to practice, exercise
1156	poseer	to possess, own
1157	proteger	to protect
1158	causar	to cause, bring about
1159	rápidamente	rapidly, quickly
1160	determinar	to determine, decide
1161	escritor	writer
1162	intento	attempt, try
1163	cobrar	to charge (money)
1164	regla	rule, ruler, regulation
1165	dividir	to divide
1166	riesgo	risk
1167	policía	police, police force, police officer
1168	inventar	to invent, make up
1169	estudiante	student
1170	plaza	square, marketplace, place, quad
1171	limitar	to limit

1172	llamada	call, knock
1173	sensación	sensation, feeling
1174	enemigo	enemy
1175	unidad	unit, unity
1176	luchar	to fight, wrestle
1177	idioma	language
1178	raíz	root
1179	compromiso	compromise, engagement
1180	comentario	remark, comment
1181	carga	load, charge, cargo
1182	marido	husband
1183	quince	fifteen
1184	constante	constant
1185	cabello	horse
1186	extremo	edge, border, end
1187	individuo	individual, person
1188	contenido	contents, content
1189	semejante	similar, such, alike
1190	obligación	obligation
1191	corte	court (f), cut (m)
1192	extranjero	foreign, alien
1193	acudir	to attend, go to, frequent
1194	daño	harm, injury, damage
1195	mensaje	message
1196	analizarto	analyze
1197	región	region
1198	evidente	evident, obvious
1199	encargar	to entrust, *se encargar*, to take charge of
1200	discusión	discussion, argument
1201	pelo	hair
1202	destinar	to assign, appoint, ordain
1203	fe	faith, *auto da fe,* act of faith, esp. martyrdom
1204	fijo	fixed, steady
1205	central	central
1206	sur	south, sometimes *sud*
1207	gesto	gesture
1208	preparado	prepared
1209	sonar	to sound, ring
1210	manifestar	to express, show
1211	controlar	to control
1212	novela	novel
1213	colegio	high school, college
1214	venta	(the) sale, *se vende*, will sell, for sale
1215	documento	document
1216	citar	to cite, quote
1217	requerir	to require
1218	moral	moral
1219	alcance	reach, scope
1220	curioso	curious, strange
1221	acaso	by chance, maybe
1222	presente	present, current

1223	inmenso	immense, vast, huge
1224	máximo	maximum
1225	crisis	crisis
1226	literatura	literature
1227	europeo	european
1228	perseguir	to persecute, pursue, chase
1229	vecino	neighbor
1230	sector	sector, area, section
1231	procurar	to try, seek
1232	perspectiva	perspective
1233	mariscos	seafood
1234	sana/sano	healthy

Okay, so there it is, a baker's thousand of words of Spanish, with some hints as to their meanings and usages. Some notes:

1.) Where the same word had more than one meaning, I may have allowed it onto the list twice.
2.) I debated whether to exclude colors and numbers, on the grounds that we had already covered those.
3.) I have made no distinction between the proper Castilian Spanish that is taught in schools and the Spanglish or Español Mexicaño that is spoken in the streets of North America.
4.) I have not always used tildes and accent markings when appropriate.
5.) Pronuciation is important.
6.) As mentioned previously, everything in and about this book is wrong, so I take no responsibility if you get punched in the nose.

Despite these issues, the vocabulary above should permit you to watch Spanish-language television or online videos and catch enough words that you can learn the rest from context. Enjoy.

FRENCH / FRANÇAIS:

Polite phrases and Important ideas:

Please	S'il vous plait (See-Voo-Play)
Thanks	Merci (MARE-see)
Thank you	Merci (MARE-see)
Thank you (emphasis)	Merci Beaucoups (MARE-see BOH-Koo)
Excuse me (interrupting)	Je m'excuse (Jim Escoose)
Pardon me (for an error)	Pardonez-moi (PAR-dohn-ay Mwah)
Pardon me (for walking in front of someone)	Pardonez-moi (PAR-dohn-ay Mwah)
Forgive me (for a grave error)	Je suis desolée (Juh Swee Day-Soh-lay)
I'm sorry	Je suis desolée (Juh Swee Day-Soh-lay)
What is your name?	Comment vous appelez-vous? (Commohn-vooz-applay-voo?)
My name is…	Je m'appelle …) (zJim-ahpell) ("I call myself…")
Where are the bathrooms?	Ou trove-ton les toilettes? (Ooo-troov-tohn lay twahletz?)

1	Un (uhn)	6	Six (Seese)	11	Onze (Ownz)
2	Deux (Dueh)	7	Sept (Set)	12	Douze (Dohz)
3	Trois (Twah)	8	Huit (Wheat)	13	Treize (Trehz)
4	Quatre (Kat)	9	Neuf (Nuhff)	14	Quatroze (KAT-OHz)
5	Cinqu(Sank)	10	Dix (Deese)	15	Quince (Kanz)
16	Seize (Seyz); dix-six (*Swiss*)	21	vingt-et-un	70	Soixante-dix
17	Dix-sept	30	Trente (Tront)	80	Quatre-vingt
18	Dix-huit	40	Quarante	90	Quatre-vingt-dix
19	Dix-neuf	50	Cinquante	100	Cent (Sawnt)
20	Vingt (Van-t)	60	Soixante	1000	Mille (Meel)

10,000	Dice Mille	1,000,000 Un Milliard	0 zero (Zeh-row)

Odd Cases and Special Phrases:

Je t'aime – *I love you.*	(Juh - Tim)
Je ne sais pas – *I don't know*	(Juhn-say-pah)
Comprendez-vous?– *Do you understand?.*	(Cahm-Prohn-Day-Voo?)
Mais oui / Mais non. *But yes / but no*	(May wee / May noh-nn)
Ta-toi! – *shut up!*	(TAH-TWAH!) (Very rude)
Venez ici – *Come here*	(VINN-ay ee-cee)

In FRENCH, sentences may be formed as Subject-Verb-Object (*Je va la*, I go there) or as Subject-Object-Verb (*Je la va*, I there go). Both cases have the same meaning. The latter construction is preferred. As in SPANISH, noun modifiers are placed after the noun (*Voiture verte*, lit. car green, not *verte voiture*, green car).

Top 1000 words:

1	de	of
2	la / le	the
3	et	and
4	les	the (plural)
5	des	of the (plural)
6	en	in, within
7	un, une	one, a
8	du, de la	of the
9	est	is, a form of *etre*, to be
10	pour	for
11	qui	who
12	dans	in, within
13	a	to
14	par	for
15	plus	more
16	pas	not
17	au	of the (singular)
18	sur	on
19	ne	not, used with *pas* or *rein*: ne ... pas did not ... , *ne fait rein*, did nothing
20	se	its
21	ce	it
22	il	he
23	sont	are
24	ou	where, or
25	avec	with
26	son	his
27	aux	of the (plural)
28	cette	that, it
29	ont	has
30	ses	their
31	mais	but
32	comme	like
33	on	one (as, a person), *on voir*, we shall see
34	nous	us, we
35	sa	her (possessive)
36	fait	does, did
37	te	you (personal-intimate)
38	aussi	also
39	leur	their, theirs
40	bien	well, fine, *j'ai bien*, I am well.
41	peut / peu	may
42	ces	it (plural)
43	y	this, it; *il y a* ... this it has: ... , (or) there is a ...
44	deux	two
45	ans	years
46	encore	again
47	n'est	isn't
48	marchons	working, going, continuing
49	donc	so, *voyons donc*! Get real, come off it, no way

50	cours	course, *de cours*, naturally
51	moins	minus, less
52	sans	without
53	C'est	it's (it is)
54	si	if, yes (in response to a negative question)
55	entre	between
56	faire	to do or to make
57	elle	she, her
58	vous	you (impersonal)
59	prix	price, prize
60	dont	of whom, of which
61	lui	him
62	effet	effect, impression
63	pays	country
64	cas	case
65	mois	month
66	taux	rate, percentage, content amount
67	annee	year
68	temps	time (i.e. clock time)
69	groupe	group
70	ainsi	as well
71	toujours	always
72	depuis	maybe
73	soit	are
74	faut	must, *Il faut que*, it must be that
75	fois	times (repetitions)
76	quelques	that which
77	sera	will be
78	entreprises	occupations, businesses
79	contre	against
80	je	I
81	beintot	last
82	etait	was
83	chez	house of
84	monde	world, *tout-le-monde*, everything or everyone
85	alors	then, so then, thus
86	sous	under
87	autres	others
88	ils	they (m)
89	reste	rest, restant, resting, from rester to rest
90	trois	three
91	non	no
92	notre	our
93	doit	must *je doit va*, I must go
94	nouveau, nouvelle,	new
95	milliards	millions
96	avant	before
97	exemple	example
98	compte	count
99	premier	first
100	terme	term, end, *mettre a terme*, to put an end to, to stop

101	avait	has
102	produits	products
103	cela	that, that one there
104	fin	end
105	niveau	level or standard, par
106	travail	work
107	partir	to part, to leave, to divide
108	trop	too, too much
109	hausse	rise, rising
110	secteur	sector, zone, area
111	part	portion, share, dividend
112	beaucoup	many or much
113	valeur	valor
114	croissance	growth
115	rapport	friendship, mutual respect
116	aujourd'hui	today
117	base	basis
118	lors	then
119	vers	against
120	souvent	often, *peu de souvent*, seldom, *le plus de souvent*, usually
121	vie	life, *vital(e)* vital, concerning life
122	frois	cold
123	autre	other
124	peuvent	they can
125	bon, bonne	good, *bons / bonnes*, material goods
126	surtout	of course, overall
127	nombre	number
128	fond	bottom, back
129	plage	beach
130	jour	day
131	va	go
132	avoir	to have
133	nos	our
134	quelque	that which
135	place	place, plaza, square, open area
136	grand	large, grand, big
137	personnes	people
138	plusieurs	several
139	certains	certain, sure
140	politique	political
141	cet	that, this one
142	chaque	each
143	chiffre	figure, number, cipher
144	devrait	must, constrained, obligated
145	rien	nothing
146	mieux	better
147	celui	that one, that he
148	qualite	quality
149	agit	(it) concerns, from *agir*, to concern, to pertain to
150	vente	sale
151	jamais	never

152	production	production
153	baisse	fall, drop
154	votre	your
155	banque	bank
156	voir / voire	to see
157	avons	we have
158	qu'un	that one
159	moment	moment
160	question	question
161	pouvoir	to be able to, to have power to
162	eleves	students
163	doute	doubt, from douter to doubt
164	petit / petite	small
165	notamment	particularly, especially noting,
166	droit	right
167	qu'elle	that she
168	heures	hours
169	cependant	hanging
170	service	service
171	Etats-Unis	United States
172	qu'ils	that they
173	action	action
174	toujours	all days, daily, always
175	celle	this
176	demande	ask, request, from *demander*, to ask, to request, to inquire
177	seront	they will have
178	economique	economical
179	raison	reason
180	nouvelles	news
181	possible	possible
182	toutefois	alltime
183	tant	so much, so many, so long
184	nouveaux	new (plural)
185	parce que	because
186	dit	said
187	vient	they came
188	jusque	right at, just at, just that
189	quatre	four
190	mise	stake, wager, interest
191	seulement	only
192	semble	together
193	vivre	to live
194	client	customer, client, guest
195	serait	they will be
196	fort /forte	strong
197	frais	fresh
198	devise	estimate
199	lieu	stead, *au lieu*, instead
200	aller	to go
201	gestion	management
202	font	fountain, source

203	gouvernement	government
204	projets	projects
205	plan	plan
206	pont	bridge, deck, point (of land)
207	outre	outer
208	pourtant	important
209	ni	neither / nor, *ni jour ni nuit* neither day nor night
210	type	person, type of person, character
211	pendant	handing
212	prendre	to take
213	actuellement	actually
214	gauche	left, (fig.) rude, uncultured, distasteful; common, garish; artistic
215	dire	to say
216	fleur	flower
217	mis	has put, from *mettre*, to place
218	parfois	sometimes
219	nom	name
220	n'ont	are not
221	veut	wants
222	present	present, current time, a gift
223	passe	passed, past, gone by
224	forme	form
225	autant	as much, as many, so much, so many
226	development	process of developing
227	mettre	to place
228	vue	seen
229	trouve	find, from *trouver*, to find
230	oeufs	eggs
231	maison	house
232	mal	bad
233	moyen	middle, *moyenne*, middle
234	doivent	they must
235	chaud	hot
236	simple	easy
237	periode	period, time, epoch; in literature, a complex work in formal French
238	enfants	children
239	assez	somewhat
240	programme	program
241	generale	general
242	eux	they, them, *eux-memes* themselves
243	semaine	week
244	tard	late
245	loi	of his
246	certaines	certain
247	savoir	to know
248	loin	later
249	explique	explained
250	plupart	most, for the larger part
251	jeunes	young (plural)
252	cinq	five
253	contrat	contract

254	seule	sole, only
255	rendement	giving
256	nombreux	numbers
257	fonction	function, work, operate
258	offre	offer, from *offrir*, to offer
259	environ	environment, circumstances, location
260	etaitent	they have been
261	recherche	research, study, investigate
262	sorte	sort, kind, type
263	suite	together, grouping
264	d'avantage	of advantage
265	bleu	blue
266	ensuite	in the room, or a room with an attached bath
267	donne	gave
268	vrai	correct, true
269	suis	am
270	aimer	to love in general, affection, romance, friendship, to like, to enjoy
271	peine	pain
272	somme, sommes	sum, sums, addition, (fig.) maths; *nous sommes*, we are
273	famille	family
274	indice	index
275	pris	taken
276	laquelle	that one which
277	gens	people
278	derniers	last ones, last bits
279	amour	love, i.e. romantic love, eros
280	afin	at the end, final, finally
281	ailleurs	somewhere else, elsewhere
282	ensemble	together
283	ventes	sells
284	rue	road, street
285	livres	books
286	vraiment	truly, truthfully
287	sein	breast
288	or	gold
289	haut, haute	high
290	porte	door
291	tel, telle	such, *rein de tel*, there's nothing like...
292	duree	endured
293	disque	disk
294	domaine	estate
295	nuit	night
296	aurait	will have
297	jeune	young
298	lorsque	when (at the time when)
299	choses	things
300	puis	then
301	aucun, aucune	to each, each
302	tandis que	while
303	coup	cut, strike, hit; stroke
304	existe	exist

305	carte	card
306	crise	crisis
307	importante	important
308	atteint	suffer (from), be afflicted with
309	revenus	income
310	montant	mounting
311	ici	here
312	s'il	if he
313	quant	how much
314	disponsible	disposible
315	rapidement	quickly
316	J'ai	I have
317	ville	town
318	mon	my
319	bas	lower, bottom, below
320	marque	mark, brand, score
321	veritable	verifiable, honest
322	ligne	line
323	longtemps	longtime, old, from old times
324	propres	proper (pl.)
325	devant	in front, in front of
326	passer	to pass, to go by, *laissez passer*, let it go, ignore it
327	depart	to leave
328	pu	could have (done)
329	total	sum
330	serie	series
331	quoi	what
332	elevee	lifted up, raised
333	connu	knew
334	principe	principal, capital
335	tendance	hearing
336	resultant	resulting (in)
337	parmi	among
338	trouver	to find
339	durant	enduring, during
340	femme, femmes	woman, women
341	desormais	from now on
342	difficile	difficult
343	autour	author
344	poste	mail, to mail, to have mailed
345	pratique	practical
346	centre	center
347	vendre	to sell
348	juillet	July
349	mai	May
350	region	region
351	sociale	social
352	filiale	of brothers
353	besoins	(they) need, from *besoir* to need
354	represente	represent
355	realite	reality

356	vaut	same, of equal quality
357	bataille	battle, fight
358	hommes	men
359	donner	to give
360	titres	titles
361	dix	ten, tenth
362	etat	state (i.e. nation, *L'Etat, c'est moi:* The State, it is me. – Louis XIV)
363	genre	kind, sort, genus
364	gros	large, huge
365	pourquoi	why, because see also *parce que,* because
366	estime	estimated
367	devient	diverting, deviating, different, outlying
368	realiser	to realize, to make real, to understand
369	creation	creation
370	semaines	weeks
371	consommation	completion
372	faible	feeble, weak
373	terrain	ground
374	droits	rights
375	puisque	since
376	facilement	easily
377	reprise	repeated
378	compris	included
379	voix	sees
380	vont	we go
381	simplement	easily, simply
382	firme	firm
383	perte	loss, damages
384	sait	know, knows
385	vite	quickly
386	via	by means of, through
387	convient	they admit
388	mot	word
389	vos	yours
390	jeu	game, play, *jeu-le-jeu-avec-moi,* humor me.
391	presque	near by, close to
392	manque	lack, shortage, deficiency
393	voiture	car
394	chef	chef, chief
395	constitue	constitutes, makes up
396	Nord	North
397	repondre	to respond
398	enfin	finally, at last, in the end
399	charge	charge
400	natur	nature
401	actuel, actuelle	actual, *actuelles,* news
402	elles	they (f)
403	membres	members
404	avaient	they have
405	gamme	musical scale, musical range
406	revanche	revenge

407	comment	how
408	gammelle	pan or dish
409	idee	idea
410	poivre	pepper
411	avenir	avenue, method, route
412	palir	to turn pale
413	creer	to create
414	concerne	concern
415	epoque	epoch, age (as unit of time), era
416	belle	beautiful
417	verre	glass
418	lequel	that which
419	cher, chere	dear, expensive; *cher ami*, dear friend, *prix cher*, expensive price
420	chacun	each one
421	lire	to read
422	decide	decided
423	mouvement	movement
424	conseil	counsel
425	necessaire	necessary
426	meilleur	better
427	celles	they
428	histoire	story
429	malgre	in spite of, *malgre tout*, after all, finally, against all odds
430	confiance	trust
431	jambe	leg
432	ayant	they had
433	papier	paper
434	commerce	commerce
435	met	put
436	contraire	contrary
437	trimestre	third of a year, one of three periods
438	jusqu'au	exactly to the, *jusqu'a l'heurre*, right on time
439	voit	he goes
440	permis	permit
441	quand	when
442	heure	time, the hour
443	guerre	war
444	acheter	to buy
445	rendre	to bring back, to return
446	ma	my
447	emploi	the job
448	main	hand
449	elements	elements
450	eau	the water
451	venir	to come
452	courant	current, trend; *au courrant*, up to date
453	suffit	suffice
454	l'ordre	the order
455	conserver	to conserve
456	que, quel, quelle	what, or that
457	largement	largely, mostly

458	soient	they are
459	deviner	to guess, to divine, to know intuitively
460	mort	dead
461	responsible	responsible
462	possibilite	possibility
463	presse	pressed
464	longue	long
465	relativement	relatively
466	moi	me
467	presence	presence
468	devraient	should
469	fumer	to smoke
470	bras	arms
471	sante	holy, sacred, blessed
472	pensees	thoughts
473	compagnie	a group, company, gathering, set of friends,
474	publique	public
475	coeur	heart
476	reponse	response
477	revenu	revenue, income
478	mesures	measures
479	nettement	definitely
480	permettre	to permit
481	ile	isle, island, *ile-de-Paris*, central Paris island featuring Notre Dame
482	retour	return
483	qu'elles	that they
484	majoritee	majority
485	moindre	to lessen
486	facile	easy
487	perdu	lost (had been lost)
488	etrangers	strangers
489	augmentee	enlarged, augmented
490	adorer	to hold in highest regard, to adore, to love as near-worship
491	taille	height, dimension, measurement
492	eviter	to avoid
493	parler	to speak, to discuss
494	propos	subject, topic, remark, point
495	proces	trial or lawsuit
496	signifie	means, signifies
497	voie	voice
498	jouer	to play
499	prevoir	to foresee
500	blanc	white; blank
501	noir	black, dark
502	logiciel	logical
503	fromage	cheese
504	continue	continued
505	bois	woods
506	marquer	to mark, to take note of, to pay attention to
507	argent	money, silver, payment
508	celui-ci	this one here

509	oeuvre	to work
510	tiers	third
511	prise	hold or catch
512	preuve	proof, evidence, *preuver* to prove
513	couleurs	colors
514	maintenant	now
515	essentiellement	essentially
516	il y a	there is
517	prevu	foreseen
518	Japon	Japan
519	centrale	central
520	yeux	eyes
521	ait	had
522	pied	foot, or floor
523	rive	bank, *rive gauche*, left bank, progressive, artful.
524	juge	judge
525	uniquement	uniquely, uncommonly, oddly
526	corps	body
527	divers	assorted, many kinds
528	reduire	reduce
529	texte	text
530	tenue	clothes, dress; *tenue de conduit* behavior
531	pression	pressure
532	mes	my (plural) *mes amis* my friends
533	n'etait	hasn't
534	style	style, mode
535	obtenir	to obtain
536	montre	to mount
537	classique	classic, classical
538	fortement	strongly
539	plein	plain
540	travailler	to work
541	credit	credit
542	directement	directly
543	prime	first, foremost
544	monnaie	money, currency, exchanges
545	precise	precise
546	appel, appelle	name, *Je m'appelle*, I call myself, *Comment vous appellez-vous?* How do you call yourself?
547	travaux	works
548	juste	exactly, precisely
549	tableau	table, scene, frozen figures
550	terre	dirt, ground, *pomme-de-terre* potato (earth-apple)
551	rouge	red
552	memoire	memory, memorial
553	partenaires	partners
554	rapide	quick
555	travailleurs	workers, workmen
556	veulent	willing
557	objectif	objective
558	il y serait	there will be
559	salle	room, hall, audience

560	parle	speak
561	musique	music
562	milieu	surroundings, environment, circumstances
563	d'entreprise	of business
564	autorites	authorities
565	chute	fall, *chute d'eau* waterfall
566	chic	fashionable, current
567	bout	end or tip
568	d'or	golden, of gold
569	lancer	to throw
570	patron	one who supports, purchaser
571	affiche	poster or flyer, *afficher* to glue on, or to attach with paste
572	situe	situated, located, placed
573	image	the image, the picture
574	etudes	studies
575	retrouve	rediscovered
576	campagne	countryside, camping, outdoors
577	hors	regarding; out of, as *hors-de-combat* unable to fight, *hors service*, out of order
578	couture	culture
579	actifs	active men
580	finalement	finally
581	achat	purchase
582	poids	pounds, or weight in general, *avoirdupois*, to have the weight (lit. to have the peas)
583	celle-ci	this here
584	entendu	hear, listen
585	investisseur	one who invests
586	mondiale	world-wide
587	accord	agreement, *d'accord*, okay, I agree
588	totalement	totally
589	clair	clear, apparent, transparent, (color) solid
590	vin	wine
591	parfaitement	perfectly
592	atteindre	to teach
593	vins	wines
594	proche	near, *proche de* near to
595	fiscale	monetary
596	Ceci	that there
597	informatique	informative
598	publicitee	publicity
599	couper	to cut
600	tenir	to hold or to keep; *tenir a droit* to keep to the right
601	l'aide	the help, the helper
602	changement	change, changes, coins
603	garantie	guarantee
604	plaisir	pleasure
605	fils	sons
606	laissez	release, or that which is released, from *laisser* to release
607	revient	cost, esp. as manufacturing cost
608	prive	private
609	magasins	magazines
610	omettre	to omit

611	peau	little
612	moteur	motor, engine
613	suivre	to follow, *suivant*, following
614	volonte	volunteered
615	beau	handsome
616	bancaire	banker
617	oublier	to forget
618	rend	return
619	affaire	affair
620	attendre	to pay attention
621	capitaux	Capitals
622	commence	start, begin
623	cree	created
624	d'eau	of water
625	devait	will have
626	d'ici	of here, from here
627	develop	developed
628	idee	idea
629	limite	limit
630	mains	hands, *main droit*, right hand, *main gauche*, left hand
631	metier	style, technique
632	prochaine	next
633	commun	shared, common, mutual
634	proprietaire	operator, owner
635	croire	to believe
636	soi	be it
637	intressant, intressante	interesting
638	reduit	reduced
639	vert	green
640	utilisateurs	users
641	sommet	top, summit, peak
642	collaboration	working together
643	consiste	consists
644	meilleurs	betters
645	consommateurs	consumers
646	l'affaire	the affair
647	contexte	context, framework, circumstances, reference frame
648	laisser	to release
649	pouvait	(they) have the power to..., (they) can
650	poste	mail or letter delivery service
651	anniversaire	birthday or anniversary of an event
652	signe	sign
653	vol	flight; theft or robbery
654	couleur	color
655	parier	to bet or to wager
656	arbre	tree
657	biere	beer
658	Mme.	abbreviation for *mademoiselle*, unmarried female (noun of address)
659	poisson	fish
660	selon	to flow, flowing
661	appartenir	to belong to... , to pertain to ...

662	remarquer	to remark
663	rater	to miss, to ruin, or to fail
664	retirer	to fall back, to retreat, to withdraw
665	bord	near, nearby, *au bord* close at hand
666	tenter	to try, to attempt
667	liberte	liberty
668	regle	ruler, means of measurement
669	merveilleux	marvelous
670	fier	proud, or to trust
671	partager	to share, to have in common, to make mutual
672	classe	class
673	dossier	file, folder, records
674	ressentir	to feel
675	bonheur	happiness
676	defendre	to defend
677	but	goal
678	bande	band, group, set of companions
679	fatiguer	to tire, to wear out, to become fatigued
680	celui-la	that one, there
681	camarade	friend or playmate
682	oiseau	bird
683	vent	wind (moving air current)
684	apprecier	to appreciate
685	systeme	system, *systeme international* the metric system
686	ferme	closed
687	fuir	to run away, escape, evade
688	ennui	boredom, esp. a profound existential weariness
689	tante	Aunt
690	dedans	within, inside
691	appartement	separately, apart, distinctly
692	bosser	to work, to endure hard labor
693	respirer	to breathe
694	entier	entire, complete, unaltered (as horses)
695	recuperer	to get back, to be refunded, to recoup
696	douleur	sadness, pain, sorrow, misery
697	grand-pere	grandfather
698	societe	society, general population, the populace; group or foundation
699	nez	nose *nez-pence* nose-pinching (glasses)
700	joie	joy
701	temoin	witness, observer
702	acteur	actor, performer, one taking action
703	moitie	half, *moitie-ferme* half closed, *moitie-prix*, half-price
704	incroyable	incredible, unbelievable, defying credence
705	bain	bath, *bain-Marie*, steam bath (bath of Mary)
706	durer	to harden, to last, to endure
707	marcher	to march
708	laver	to wash
709	dent	tooth
710	la-dedans	in there
711	mademoiselle	Miss (as a noun of address); unmarried young woman or girl
712	adresse	address, to address, to speak to, home location

713	riche	rich, *nouveau riche*, uncultured (newly rich)
714	sonner	to ring
715	chaussure	belt
716	oreille	ear
717	grand-mere	grandmother
718	ancien	ancient
719	inutile	useless, broken
720	ravir	to delight
721	blague	joke, *blague-a-part*, no joke, seriously
722	avenir	future
723	maniere	way, *maniere de tout*, anyway
724	traverser	to go across, to go sideways, to trek
725	cour	court, courtyard
726	retenir	to retain, to keep, to hold on to
727	liste	list
728	remonter	to come back up, to go back to the top, to put back together
729	coucher	to lie down
730	moquer	to mock
731	etudier	to study
732	installer	to install
733	secours	help, first aid, cf. *m'aidez*, help me
734	proposer	to offer to do, to propose or suggest; to intend
735	inspecteur	inspector, police detective
736	mignon	dear, also *mignonne*, dear, compare *filet mignon*, the dearest cut
737	probablement	probably
738	risque	risk
739	ange	angel
740	avance	advance (as movement, or as timing)
741	langue	language, tongue, dialect
742	colere	anger, *colere contra* angry with
743	gorge	throat, *engorger*, to swallow, to engulf, to consume
744	engager	to engage, to fight, to connect
745	voleur	thief
746	cesser	to stop, to cease, to quit
747	tort	wrong, fault, offense
748	signifier	signify, mean, convey, report
749	reparer	to repair
750	construire	to construct, (fig.) to construe
751	pain	bread, pan grille toast
752	chien	dog, *un mal de chien*, a lot of trouble
753	horrible	horrible, evoking horror
754	profiter	to make a profit, to accrue benefit
755	pierre	rock, outcropping, large stone, monument, boulder
756	pleuvoir	to rain, to precipitate, *il pleut* it's raining
757	clé	key
758	tantot	sometimes, this afternoon
759	glace	ice, ice cream
760	separer	to separate
761	sept	seven
762	maladie	Illness, sickness, disease
763	quartier	living space, quarters, neighborhood

764	desirer	to desire
765	travers	across, sideways, crossing, to go across
766	respecter	to respect, to regard, *a respect de* with respect to
767	tas	pile or heap
768	enfuir	to run away, to escape, to evade
769	diriger	to lead, to direct, to steer, to make one's way (towards...)
770	crever	to burst, to go flat, (fig.) to die
771	poursuivre	to chase, to pursue, to seek, to go after
772	eglise	church building, cathedral
773	directeur	one who directs, leader, movie creator
774	forcer	to force, to break (as a lock)
775	bombe	spray
776	je, j'	I, *je suis*, I am, *j'accuse*, I accuse, *je m'excuse*, I excuse myself
777	espoir	to hope, *sans espoir*, hopeless
778	tuer	to kill
779	grandir	to enlarge
780	Dimanche	Sunday
781	bateau	boat, ship
782	sac	bag, sack
783	impossible	impossible
784	seconde	second of time, a moment, compare *deuxeme*, second (ordinal)
785	decouvrir	to discover, find
786	erreur	error, mistake
787	soleil	sun, sunlight
788	voyage	trip, journey
789	sauter	to jump
790	rever	to dream
791	detester	to hate, detest
792	faux	wrong, false, fallacious
793	balle	bullet, ball (sports equipment), dot
794	empecher	to prevent
795	maintenir	to keep, maintain
796	cheveu	a hair
797	sujet	subject, topic, theme
798	supposer	to suppose, assume
799	tranquille	quiet, calm
800	neuf	nine
801	espouser	to marry, to espouse; (fig.) to support an idea
802	arrondisement	district
803	toute	everything, all
804	agent	officer, oficial, agent
805	approcher	to approach
806	sens	sense, senses, meaning; *en cet sens* in that way
807	craindre	to fear, to be afraid of
808	six	six
809	crier	to shout
810	inviter	to invite
811	reflechir	to reflect, think
812	espece	species, kind
813	arranger	to arrange, to organize
814	naitre	to be born

815	allo	hello (informal, used with telephone)
816	hote	host
817	soupcon	suspicion
818	hotel	hotel, guesthouse, inn
819	debut	beginning
820	souffrir	to be in pain, suffer
821	remercier	to thank
822	choix	choice, selection
823	securite	safety, security
824	avocat	lawyer, advocate, defender, advisor
825	attraper	to catch
826	envoyer	to dispatch
827	peuple	people
828	dame	lady, queen
829	verifier	to check, verify
830	abandonner	to abandon, leave, desert
831	journal	newspaper, diary, journal
832	serieux	genuine, serious
833	bruler	to burn
834	loi	law, rule
835	fric	(slang) money, cash, liquid assets
836	situation	situation; job; location
837	sauf	except, save for this
838	accident	accident
839	soldat	soldier
840	amoureux	loving
841	assurer	to assure, insure
842	humain	human
843	mer	sea, seaside; *cel de mer* sea salt
844	victime	victim, casualty
845	completement	completely, fully, in depth
846	garde	guard; caregiver, nurse
847	meurtre	murder
848	traiter	to treat; to deal with; to pay or pay back.
849	doucement	gently, softly, sweetly
850	blesser	to injure, wound, hurt, *blessure*, injury, wound
851	colonel	colonel
852	voici	here is, here are, this is, these are, cf. *voila* (*voici la*), here it is
853	acquérir	to acquire
854	convenir	to come together, to agree, to be suitable, to join
855	procéder	to proceed
856	examiner	to examine
857	soin	care
858	mesurer	to measure
859	traitement	treatment, salary, wage
860	Jeudi	Thursday
861	impliquer	to imply, implicate
862	logique	logic, logical
863	individu	individual
864	donnée	fact, a single datum, a bit of information
865	demi	half

866	combattre	to fight
867	suivant	following, *et les suivant*, and those following
868	mériter	to deserve, to merit, to be worthy of
869	emprunter	to borrow
870	comporter	to consist, to include, to be composed of, to behave or to carry oneself
871	sang	blood
872	millier	a thousand or so, compare *mille*, thousand
873	emporter	to take, to remove, to lose one's temper; *emporter ou*, to blow away,
874	nucléaire	nuclear
875	traduire	to translate
876	vif	lively
877	doubler	to double, to overtake, to reverse one's course
878	Février	February
879	mode	mode, way, fashion, style
880	industriel	industrial
881	honneur	honor
882	vaste	vast, immense
883	évoquer	to recall, evoke
884	tendre	to tighten; extend, stretch; (tender)
885	étape	stage (of a process), step
886	physique	physical, (physics)
887	accuser	to accuse
888	méthode	method, means, pattern, system; *methode champagnoise* sparkling wine from America
889	fonctionner	to function, work
890	envers	towards
891	distribuer	to distribute, give out
892	prétendre	to pretend
893	professeur	professor, teacher
894	chaîne	chain, channel
895	dommage	damage, harm; *c'est dommage*, too bad
896	version	version
897	règlement	rule, regulation
898	relatif	relative
899	Mercredi	Wednesday
900	sinon	otherwise, or else, if not
901	entreprendre	to begin, start, undertake
902	au-delà	beyond
903	étendre	to spread out, stretch out, extend
904	profond	deep, profound
905	décrire	to describe
906	récent	recent
907	télévision	television
908	retraite	retirement, pension
909	sortir	to exit, to part ways, to go out *voulez-vous sortir avec moi?* Will you go out with me?
910	frontière	border, frontier
911	égal	equal, *liberte, egality, fraternite*, freedom, equality, and brotherhood
912	promesse	promise
913	entretenir	to maintain
914	habiter	to live, inhabit
915	art	art
916	accueillir	to welcome, greet, accommodate

917	libérer	to free, liberate, release
918	vivant	alive, living
919	université	university
920	rire	to laugh
921	crainte	fear
922	commettre	to commit
923	précisément	precisely
924	soutien	support, *soutenir*, to support, *la soutenir*, to support that
925	facilement	easily
926	urgence	emergency, urgency
927	salopette	overalls (garment)
928	portefeuille	wallet
929	Juin	June
930	vitesse	life, life-force, livelihood
931	derriere	behind, in back of, (fig.) backside
932	tot	early
933	retarder	to slow down, to reduce speed, to restrict
934	jolie	pretty
935	termine	ended
936	gentille	gentle
937	descendre	to descend, to come down
938	felicitations	greetings, congratulations, joyful declarations
939	oeil	eye
940	asseoir	to sit down
941	cerveau	brain
942	coupable	guilty, responsible, held accountable
943	tombe	grave
944	sentir	to sense, especially to feel, to smell, to taste
945	eclater	to spread, to open, to part
946	gagner	to win, to earn, to achieve
947	enquete	poll, vote, survey
948	ramener	to take back, to reduce
949	drogue	drug
950	toillettes	public bathrooms, lavatories
951	pleurer	to cry
952	mienne	mine
953	couteau	knife
954	retrecir	to shrink
955	gout	taste, fashionability, propriety, *bon gout* good taste, tasteful
956	detruire	to destroy
957	choisir	to choose
958	fermer	to close
959	flingue	gun
960	doigts	fingers
961	ondulation	a wave
962	raison, raisons	reason, thought; reasoning, contemplation
963	Samedi	Saturday
964	bouteille	bottle
965	gare	train station
966	frapper	to shake, to strike
967	amuser	to amuse, to interest

968	montagne	mountain
969	souhaiter	to wish
970	hasard	hazard, danger
971	aveugle	blind
972	obliger	to oblige, to require; *je suis oblige,* I am indebted (to you)
973	viande	food, edibles, groceries
974	neige	snow
975	gateau	cake
976	chat	cat
977	dortoir	dormitory
978	gaz	gas, fumes, natural gas, propane
979	cacher	to hide, to store, to conceal, *cachet* something hidden
980	visage	face
981	naissance	birth, development (of)
982	volontre	to volunteer
983	recevoir	to receive
984	charmant	charming, delightful
985	chercher	to search
986	conduit	to conduct
987	parvenir	to reach
988	aeroport	airport
989	poulet	chicken
990	nerveaux	nervous
991	apporter	to carry (away)
992	sage	wise
993	ombre	shade, darkness, umbra; (fig.) ghost
994	vache	cow, cf. *boeuf,* beef
995	foret	forest
996	paquet	parcel, package, packet
997	ouverte	to open, *ouvertement* openly, in public, overtly
998	dormir	to sleep
999	vole	will, intent, purpose, plan
1000	chemise	shirt
1001	billet	ticket, bill (i.e. handbill, flyer)
1002	penser	to think
1003	tete	head
1004	reparer	repair, retire, move back,
1005	lecon	lesson
1006	relancer	to throw back or restart
1007	facture	invoice or bill
1008	devoiler	to reveal, to uncloak
1009	freiner	to slow down, to apply brakes
1010	debarquer	to land, to unload, to go ashore
1011	loger	to lodge, to accommodate
1012	grandeur	greatness, largeness, immense scale
1013	blesse	wounded
1014	etoile	star
1015	attelage	hook
1016	fidele	loyal, faithful
1017	foi	faith
1018	marche	market, *supermarche* supermarket

1019	otite	infection
1020	jaunir	to turn yellow
1021	embarder	to swerve, to turn aside
1022	penible	difficult
1023	gourde	water bottle
1024	depasser	to overtake, *depasse* overtaken
1025	jeter	to throw *jetee* thrown (overboard, thrown away)
1026	graisse	fat, grease alt. *gras, grasse* fat, *Mardi gras* Fat Wednesday (start of Lent)
1027	potable	drinkable
1028	abat-jour	awning, screen, sunshade
1029	chaux	limestone, chalk
1030	jupe	skirt
1031	lisse	smooth, from *lisser*, to smooth or hone
1032	deforme	bent, deformed, misshapen
1033	natte	braid
1034	paisable	peaceful, peacable, peace-seeking
1035	passerelle	footbridge
1036	bobine	spool
1037	frustre	frustrated
1038	parasol	sun shade
1039	midi	noon
1040	garer	to park
1041	nuit	night
1042	sang-froid	self control, lit. cold blood
1043	gauffre	waffle
1044	arriere	backwards
1045	provoquer	to cause, to bring about, to provoke
1046	arrondir	to round off
1047	huile	oil
1048	ecluse	to lock
1049	selon	according to
1050	minuit	midnight
1051	empaqueter	to pack
1052	pendule	clock, pendulum, swinging weight
1053	littoral	coast
1054	deranger	to disturb *ne deranger pas*, do not disturb
1055	macon	bricklayer, mason
1056	para-pluie	umbrella
1057	Savoir-Faire	to know what to do, sophistication, calmness under stress

Okay, that's about 1000 words of French, plus or minus 5.7%, more or less. Some notes:

1. Accent marks are a pain to replicate, so they've been largely ignored here. If that's a major problem, look up the word elsewhere and note the accent marks.

2. So, is *d'Or* (golden) a different word from *Or* (gold)? Well, in that case, I said yes, and allowed two entries. In other cases – in most cases – I did not. It is a peculiarity of French that nearly any word starting with a vowel or with H can have l' or d' stuck to the front of it. It changes the meaning a little, but you should be able to figure it out. Also, many words appear more than once due to different forms, especially in verbs.

3. Word frequency is a little bit inconsistent in French as well, because the possible corpus varies widely over time. Yes, there is a strong movement to keep French static, but the French of Tolstoy is not the French of Voltaire, and the French of Camus is not the French of Tolstoy. Words go in and out of fashion. In short, the word order given here is my best possible estimation. The words have not changed, but the frequencies may change.

4. In the above list you will see several variants of *voulet*, to want. One should note that *je veux* is a rather strong form of the idea; it is "I want" but suggests that "I demand" or "I insist upon." When requesting something politely, one should say *Je voudrais*, "I would like." You might ask someone *voulez-vous sortir avec moi?* (Do you want to go out with me?). But you would say *Je voudrais sortir avec vous* (I would like to go out with you) instead of *je veux sortir avec vous* (I want to go out with you). One does wish to respect the other party's free will, after all. *Voudrais* and its variants do not appear on the above lists, hence this note.

5. In the same sense, one should reserve *tu, te,* and *ton,* (you, you, yours) which are very familiar, for those with whom one is emotionally close. A romantic partner, a close friend, a family member – these deserve *tu.* In all other circumstances, use *vous* and *votre.*

6. I have neutered most of the words. In actual French grammar, nouns are masculine or feminine. Verbs and adjectives can be gendered also. But the point of this book is to NOT make you memorize complex conjugations. When you start to apply these words by watching TV and movies in French, or by reading in French, you will quickly learn that *je suis,* but *tu es, vous etes, il est, elle est, ils sont, elles sont, nous sommes,* and so forth. This book is not intended to teach grammar, beyond what is absolutely unavoidable.

7. French pronunciation is a subject unto itself. As a general rule, most sounds are meant to be slightly nasal. Past tense verbs typically end in an –ay sound. So do many (most) infinitive verbs. And so do most first-person singular verbs. Finally, terminal consonants are usually not voiced (or faintly voiced): *Comment* (how) usually sounds like CAWmahn(t). The exception is a following word beginning with a vowel, as with *Comment allez-vous?* (how go you?, how are you?) which sounds like CAWmahn-TALLAY-voo. That terminal T migrates to the next word. Why, you ask? That's a good question…

8. Congratulatory messages oddly seem to mean exactly the opposite of what they should mean. *Bein Fait!* does not mean (as one might assume) that you are impressed with a person's accomplishments, but rather, that they have somehow really messed it up this time. The "Well done" is usually given with extreme irony, apparently. Likewise, one should avoid any kind of congratulatory message until one is certain of how it is typically used, and of how the recipient will understand it.

SERBO-CROAT:

Polite phrases and Important ideas:

Please — Molimo Vas
Thanks — Hvala
Thank you — Hvala Vam
Thank you (emphasis) — Mnogo Vam Hvala

Excuse me (interrupting) — Izgovor
Pardon me (for an error) — Izvinite
Pardon me (for walking in front of someone) — Izvinite
Forgive me (for a grave error) — Oprosti Mi
I'm sorry — Žao Mi Je

What is your name? — Kako Se Zoveš?
My name is… — Moje Ime Je

Where are the bathrooms? — Gde Su Kupatila?

Is there a taxi-stand near here? — Postoji Li Blizu Taksi Stajalište?

How do you spell that, please? — Kako To Pišete Molim Vas?

Have you read the Rex Stout book, *The Black Mountain?* — Jeste Li Pročitali Knjigu Rek Stout *Crna Planina?*

1	Jedna	6	Šest	11	Jedanaest
2	Dva	7	Sedam	12	Dvanaest
3	Tri	8	Osam	13	Trinaest
4	Četiri	9	Devet	14	Četrnaest
5	Pet	10	Deset	15	Petnaest

16	Šesnaest	21	Dvadeset jedan	70	Sedamdeset
17	Sedamnaest	30	Trideset	80	Osamdeset
18	Osamnaest	40	Četrdeset	90	Devedeset
19	Devetnaest	50	Pedeset	100	Stotinu
20	Dvadeset	60	Šezdeset	1000	Hiljada

10,000 Deset hiljada   1,000,000 Milion   1,000,000,000 Milijarde   0 Nula

1	je	is
2	da	that
3	ne	not
4	se	you
5	to	it
6	sam	alone, by himself
7	što	what
8	na	on the
9	ti	you, also *vas, vama, vi, tebe, tee*
10	si	you are
11	mi	me, we, ourselves
12	za	for
13	li	you
14	ja	I, myself, me
15	su	are
16	ali	but
17	nije	is not
18	me	me, this person
19	i	and
20	te	thee
21	ovo / ovu / ova	this
22	samo	only, merely
23	bi	to
24	kako	how, by what means, what about, as
25	od	of, with, from the
26	ce	will
27	sa	with, from after
28	dobro	farm, also well or fine (good), *za tvoje dobro*, for your own good
29	smo	we, we are
30	ako	if
31	sve	all, everything
32	cu	shall
33	kao	as
34	tako	so, thus, in such a way
35	znam	I know
36	biti	to be, to exist,
37	ovdje	here, in here, at this point
38	nisam	I am not
39	mogu	can
40	ste	you are
41	bio	was
42	zašto	why
43	još	else, even, more, still
44	pa	well, so, then
45	nešto	something
46	redu	OK
47	on	he
48	bilo	pulse
49	koji	who
50	vas	your, yours
51	kad /a	when

52	ih	them
53	mislim, misli	he thinks
54	hvala	Thank, Thanks, Thank you, Thanks to
55	iz	from
56	znaš	you know
57	ima	have
58	gdje	where, whereabouts, whither
59	možda	maybe, perhaps, possibly
60	šta	what
61	ili	or
62	vam	to you
63	više	more, longer
64	sada	presently
65	moj, moja, moje, moji, moju	my, also *mojem, mojih, mojoj, mojom*
66	rekao	said
67	bih	should
68	do	to, by, till
69	nas	our
70	cemo	we will
71	mu	he, him
72	onda /e	then
73	nema	no
74	tko	who
75	zar	right
76	ništa /e /i /o /u	nothing
77	mene, meni	me
78	želim	I want
79	tebe	you
80	ceš	you'll, will, wish, desire
81	bila	been
82	molim	please
83	možeš, mozete	you can
84	sad	present, now
85	može	can
86	tamo	there, over there
87	imam	I have a
88	jesi	are
89	hajde	come on! Go ahead!
90	tu	here
91	ni	nor
92	hej	Hey!
93	ona	she
94	nam /a	us
95	vi	you
96	reci	say
97	prije	before, preferably
98	svi	all, all of
99	nisi	not
100	idemo	here we go
101	zbog	cause of
102	ljude, ljudi, ljudima	people

103	treba	should, shall
104	jer	because
105	moram	I have to
106	po	per
107	jedan	one
108	koliko	how much
109	zato	therefore, thus
110	misliš	you mean, you think so
111	baš	just so, exactly, precisely
112	stvarno	really, downright, substantially, fairly
113	vec	already, yet
114	uvijek	always, whenever
115	gospodina /e	sir
116	nece	will not
117	nego	him
118	bez	without
119	stvari	things, stuff, belongings
120	dok	while
121	možemo, mož	husband
122	imaš	you have
123	koje /kojem	that
124	vrijeme	time, season
125	želiš	gel, want
126	ok	OK
127	taj	that
128	toga	that
129	ovaj	this, this one
130	daj	come on
131	tvoj /a /e /i /u	yours
132	imamo	we have
133	ono	it, that
134	nemoj	do not
135	moramo	we must
136	nikad /a	never
137	oni	they
138	žao	evil, *za* yeah
139	bar, barem	at least, if only, at any rate
140	posao	job, work
141	znaci	means
142	tome	it
143	mogao, mogla, mogli, moglo	could
144	naravno	of course
145	joj	her
146	koja /kojeg /a	which
147	dan /a /as /e /i /u	day
148	moraš, morate, morati	you have, you have to, have to
149	put /a	time, times
150	bolje /a /i /u	better
151	rad /a /e /i /ili /ila /im	work /work /they work /works /worked /worked /I'm working
152	godina /e /u	Year, *godina ma*, elderly, *koliko mu je godina*, how old is he?
153	necu	I will not

154	hoceš /ete	wants
155	dobar	Good, pleasant
156	im	them
157	radiš	doing, operating
158	kod	code
159	dva	two
160	mislila, mislili, mislio	thought
161	izgleda	apparently, it seems
162	mora, moraju,	must
163	bili	were
164	netko	someone
165	život	life
166	rekla	she said
167	vidim	I see.
168	evo	here, here is
169	svoje	their
170	tata /e /i	Dad, Daddy
171	nisu	they are not
172	vremena	time, times
173	vidio	saw, seen
174	stvar	thing, matter, cause, agree
175	njega	him
176	volim	I love
177	vidjeti	to see, observe, perceive
178	mama, mame, mami, mamu	Mom, *mamom* Mommy
179	odmah	now, right now
180	imao	had
181	jako	very, strongly, deeply, intensely
182	neka	let
183	zdravo	honey, hi, soundly, hello
184	ime /imenom /imenu	name
185	znate	you know
186	idem	I am going to
187	zna	knows
188	cemu	what
189	tri	three
190	pomoci	help, assist
191	trebao	need, suppose, necessary
192	kuci	home
193	bit	essence, bitan, essential
194	jeste	it is
195	covjek /a /e /i /o /u /om	man
196	tobom	you
197	nitko	nobody
198	ici	to go
199	jesam	yes, I am.
200	mnoge, mnogi, mnogo	many
201	vrlo	very
202	upravo	just, right, timely
203	cekaj, cekajte	hang on, wait, hold it
204	kojoj /koju /kome	whom

205	dogodilo	happened
206	tim	team
207	opet	again, anew, now and then
208	kažem	I say
209	želi	he wants, he wishes to
210	kaže	says
211	svoj	its own
212	neka /e /i /o /u /ih /im /om	some
213	cete	will
214	svoju	my, mine
215	vidi	see
216	mnom	me
217	nismo	we
218	toliko	that much, insofar
219	znao	knew
220	ide	goes
221	oko	eye
222	bude	is
223	prema	according to, per
224	tebi	to you
225	idi /idite	go
226	žena	woman
227	jednom	once
228	cak	even
229	ovde	here
230	vrata	the door, portal
231	nemam	I have not
232	god	Year, *godina ma*, elderly, *koliko mu je godina,* how old is he?
233	htio /hteo	wanted
234	pogledaj	look at
235	vidimo	we see
236	otac	father, old man
237	vidiš	you see
238	hocu	I will
239	ta	yes, this
240	ovamo	here
241	mjesto, mjestu	place, *mjesta* places
242	prvi	principal, leading, prime, first
243	dovoljno	enough, sufficiently, amply
244	drugi	second, other, another
245	covjece	man
246	postoji	exist, since then
247	dodi	come
248	oprosti	sorry, forgive, pardon
249	došao	came
250	novac	money
251	ove	these
252	dušo	honey, possibly shower
253	slušaj	listen, obey
254	putem /u	through, via, way
255	imate	you have a

256	odavde	from here
257	no	than
258	njih	them
259	uciniti	do
260	dogada	events, happens, happenings
261	drago	expensive
262	znati	knowing
263	lijepo, lijepa, lijepe, lijepi, lijep	beautiful, pretty, nice,
264	naci	find
265	bok	side, torso, hip, flank
266	dosta	enough, quite, satisfying
267	doci	come, arrive, turn up, conveniently nearby
268	oprostite	I beg your pardon
269	siguran	sure, safe, secure
270	dobra /e /i /ih /im /u	good, well, farm
271	sutra	tomorrow
272	sebe	yourself
273	ubiti	kill
274	kog /koga	whom
275	ma	at all, whatsoever
276	nakon	after
277	nacin	the way
278	kroz	through, out of, across
279	ko	who
280	gore	above, up, upstairs, overhead, aloft
281	pravu	rights
282	neceš /te	you will not
283	mala /e /i /im /o /u	small
284	cula /i, cuo,	heard
285	unutra	in, inside
286	dugo	long
287	brzo	quickly
288	cini	makes
289	ju	it, he
290	vratiti	restore, pay back
291	jedna	one
292	ova	this, this one
293	zajedno	together
294	pod	floor, beneath, below
295	svaka /e /i /o	every, seamstress
296	tocno	exactly, accurately
297	otici	depart, push off
298	trebam	I need, I need to
299	noc	night
300	nekoliko	several, some, fewest
301	njim	it
302	želite	you want
303	dalje	further
304	vaš	your, yours
305	osim	except, aside from
306	auta /o /u	passenger car

307	raditi	work, labor
308	ubio	killed
309	imati	have
310	pravo	law, right, directly
311	jes	yes
312	pomoc	help
313	previše	overly, too much
314	minut, minuta, minute, minutu	minute, minutes
315	vama	to you
316	napraviti	to make
317	protiv	against
318	par	pair, couple, twosome
319	veceras	tonight, this evening
320	loše	bad
321	kažeš	you say
322	nadam	I hope
323	mrtav /a /e /i	dead
324	svida	like, likes
325	isto /u	also
326	trebali	need
327	teško	heavy, hard, thick
328	van	out, without, outward
329	prvo	first, foremost
330	razgovarati	talk
331	dolje	down
332	ovako	like this, this kind of
333	trebalo	should
334	tom	that
335	dio	part, portion, share
336	ovog /a /e /i /o /u	this, of this
337	pusti	let go
338	znamo	we know
339	dvije	two
340	jedne	one, *jednosta* oneness, integrity
341	istina /e /u	truth
342	tip	type
343	imaju	they have
344	prava /e /i /o /u	rights
345	jednim /jednog /a /jednoj /jednu	one, single, some
346	poput	like, in the style of
347	budi, budite	be, to be
348	misle, mislite	think, *misliti* to think
349	broj	number, numeral, figure
350	zove	call
351	dijete	child
352	ovom	this, this one
353	mog, moga	my
354	vjerujem	I believe
355	sto	table
356	vjerovati	to believe, credit
357	naše /g /m	our, us, ourselves

358	onaj	that, that one
359	gde	where
360	kasnije	later
361	prijatelj	friend, companion
362	kakav	what
363	uz	up, with, along
364	dolazi	coming
365	preko	over, out of, on, through
366	rekli	they said
367	zapravo	actually, possibly jar
368	dobiti	obtain, receive, or gain
369	ucinio	did, done
370	vjerojatno	probably, likely
371	bismo	we would
372	njegov /a /e /i /ih /im /o /og /oj /om /u	him
373	star /a /e /i /o /u	old
374	napravio	did
375	poslije	afterwards
376	veliki	large
377	brod, broda	ship, *na brodu*, aboard ship, *brodova*, ships
378	pet	five
379	života /e	life
380	hoce	will, want, wish
381	dao	gave, given
382	tog	this
383	iza	behind
384	ideš	are you going?, going
385	bog /a /u	God, gods, deity, divinity, *Hvala Bogu!* Thank God!
386	one	they
387	jednostavno	simply
388	kuca, kuce, kucu	house
389	nekoga /me	someone
390	razumijem	I see
391	gotov /i /o	over, finished, ready, complete, prepared
392	dati	given, give away
393	vrati	return back
394	imala /i /o	had
395	dolara	dollars
396	govori	speaks
397	prestane /i /ite	stop, cut it out, cease, desist
398	veze	relations
399	došli	welcome
400	otišao	had gone
401	novi	new
402	dakle	therefore
403	ostat	the rest
404	želio	wished
405	trebala	should
406	gledaj	look, watch
407	problema	problem
408	njima	to them

409	drži		hold it
410	sin		son
411	momci, momka, momke		guys
412	uzmi		take it
413	trebaš		need you, you need
414	drugo		other
415	natrag		back, backwards, behind, reverse
416	važno		serious, important
417	majci, majka /e /o /om /u		mother
418	posla		deal, business
419	vidjela /i		saw, seen
420	sati		hours
421	spreman		ready, prepared
422	dobio		received
423	zaista		really, truly
424	svojim		my, its
425	pazi		watch out
426	srca /e /u		heart
427	briga		trouble, worry
428	vaša /e /i		your, yours
429	pitanje		the question
430	trenutak	a	moment, the moment, instant
431	njemu		him
432	oružja		weapon, weapons, tools, hardware
433	osjecam		I feel
434	veoma		very, vastly
435	ipak		however, still, but, yet, though, nevertheless
436	trebamo		we need
437	nju		her
438	prica /u		story, narrative
439	jutra /o		morning
440	ovim		with this
441	žene		women, see *gospoda, lena, dama, dame*
442	sat		clock, hour
443	moci		be able, *moc* power
444	odlicno		great, unparalleled
445	cijela /e /i /o		whole, complete, full
446	svog		his, of his
447	nemaš		you do / you do not have
448	uopce		at all, in general
449	sebi		themselves
450	jasno		clear, plain, distinct
451	svijet		world, crowd, spirit
452	tada		then, afterwards
453	uskoro		soon, presently
454	jel		right
455	vezi		ties, embroider
456	ponovo		anew, afresh, again
457	našao		found, discovered
458	obitelj		family
459	najbolja /e /i /ih		best, good, fine, benign

460	glavu	head, headpiece, noggin,
461	prijatelja /e /i	friends
462	jedina	only, sole, single, one
463	volio	loved
464	cega	which
465	oci	eyes
466	valjda	maybe, I guess
467	budem	I
468	skoro	soon, recently, almost
469	voli	loves, likes
470	bratic	cousin
471	morao	had, had to
472	jest	is
473	znala	knew
474	oca	father
475	nekog /oj	some
476	cudan, cudn /a /e /i /o /u	strange, unusual, odd, eccentric
477	potpuno	completely, entirely
478	nemamo	we do not have
479	kraj	the end, last, finish, terminus
480	grad	town or city
481	necemo	we will not
482	pred	in front of, towards
483	sata	hour, clock
484	vidite	you see
485	ženu	woman
486	gospodo	Gentlemen
487	lako, laku, lagano	easy
488	tek	only
489	sama /e /i	alone, mere
490	polako	slowly
491	stalno	constantly
492	sjajno	great, superbly, magnificently
493	njom	it
494	pištolj	handgun
495	kamo	where to
496	životu	life
497	žele	want, zel wish
498	decko	boy
499	bliže /u	near, close by, also *bližak*; see *bliži* nearer,
500	ozbiljna /e /o /i /u	serious, grave, severe
501	sretan	happy, fortunate
502	rijec	word, speech
503	velika /e	big
504	izmedu	between, among, inter-
505	svijetu	world
506	strane	sides
507	cetiri	four
508	biste /ar	clear, transparent, *bistariti se*, to clear up
509	pola	half
510	svih	all, of all

511	kažu	they say
512	umrijeti	to die
513	takoder	also, as well
514	sigurna /i /o	certain, confident
515	noci	night
516	mom	my
517	negde / negdje	somewhere
518	ikada	ever
519	radije	rather
520	kakva	how
521	znaju	they know
522	radite	performing, operating
523	decki	boys
524	zvuci	sounds
525	smrt	death
526	ljubav, ljubavi	love
527	vani	outside
528	sjecaš	you remember
529	radimo	we are working
530	voliš	you love
531	ponekad	sometimes
532	druge	other
533	vratio	returned
534	uzeti	take
535	niti	they are not
536	cujem, cuješ, cujete, cuti	hear
537	budeš	you will be
538	pronaci	find, locate, discover
539	brat, brata, brate	brother, *bratski*, fraternal
540	došla	came
541	osoba /e /i /o /u	person, human,
542	slucaj	case, the case
543	ponovno	again
544	spremni	ready
545	pretpostavljam	I guess, presumption
546	govoriš	talking about, you're talking
547	izgledaš	you look
548	jesu	they did
549	smrti	death
550	živi	lives
551	našla /e /i /o	found, discovered
552	moguce	possible, *mogucnost* possibility, *mogucnosti* opportunities
553	nemojte	don't
554	ovoj	this, this one
555	ideja /e /u	ideas
556	pojma	idea, concept
557	rat /a /u	war, installment, ration
558	vodi	leads, water, take, deep
559	lice, licu	face, *lica* faces
560	ostani /te	stay
561	ikad	and when

562	dvoje	two
563	manje	less
564	drag /a /i	dear, darling, nice, precious
565	pre	before
566	bojim	I fear
567	govorim	I speak
568	izgubila /i /izgubio	lost, misplaced
569	sina	rail, brace, track
570	pitam	asking
571	odakle	from where
572	prijatelju	friend
573	šest	six
574	pitanja /i	questions
575	djevojka /e /om /u	a girl /girls /girl /girl
576	tvog	your, of yours
577	slucaju	case, occurence
578	sjecam	I remember
579	recite	the words
580	tjedan	weekly
581	prilicno	pretty, sufficiently
582	kraju	in the end, ending
583	policija /e /i /o /u	police
584	uvek	always, ever
585	doma	home
586	san	sleep, dream,
587	svega	everything
588	daleko	far
589	svima	everyone, to all
590	ispod	below, beneath, down below, sub-, under
591	vode	water
592	pricati	to talk
593	pricaš	talking about
594	cudi	surprising
595	novca	money
596	nazad	back
597	šanse	chances
598	jedino	solely
599	soba /e /i /u /nim	room
600	razlog	reason, motive, excuse
601	krv, krvi	blood
602	svom	his, to his
603	morat	you
604	obitelji	family
605	umro	died
606	ovome	to this
607	zaboravi	forget, *zaborav* oblivion, *zabor* fence
608	mrzim	I hate
609	djeca /e /i /o /u	children
610	želimo	we want
611	cim	as soon as, immediately upon
612	naprijed	forward

613	sine	son
614	tijelo	torso, figure, body, flesh
615	smiješno	funny
616	sinoc	last night
617	pokušavam	I am trying
618	ranije	earlier, formerly, previously
619	otrov /a /e /i /o /u	poison, toxin, venom
620	poruka /e /i /o /u	message, messages
621	nje	one
622	pogledajte	look
623	uradio	done
624	dode	comes
625	pitati	ask, query, interogate
626	ujutro	in the morning
627	ovi	these, this one
628	tražim	I'm looking for
629	drugog	another
630	zovem	I'm calling
631	uzeo	took
632	dame	ladies
633	barem	at least
634	bol, boli	pain or ache
635	rijeci	words
636	njoj	her
637	zanima	interested, *zanim* before
638	lud, luda, ludi, ludo, ludak	crazy, demented, mad; madly, fervently, senselessly
639	nikoga	no one
640	desilo	happened
641	pokušao	tried, attempted
642	doista	really, indeed
643	nekako	somehow
644	vreme	time, season, weather
645	gradu	city
646	pice	drink, drinks, thirst-quencher
647	živjeti	to live
648	time	thereby
649	sva	all, every, seam
650	zemlju	bun
651	igra	game, play, act, sport, recreation
652	razumiješ	understands
653	takav	such, such that
654	smiri	calm down
655	živ	alive
656	oboje	both of you
657	divno	wonderful, delightful
658	gledati	watch
659	uredu	device
660	svim	all
661	kakve /i /u	what
662	ostali /o	others, residual, remainder
663	zvao	called

664	brže	faster
665	vašu	your, yours
666	pitao	he asked
667	zemlji	bunny, buns
668	ostavio	left
669	deset	ten
670	ostaviti	to leave
671	mir, mira, miru	peace
672	pored	next to, alongside
673	dogoditi	happen, befall, perchance occurs
674	isti	same
675	doktore	Doctor
676	razloga	causes, reasons
677	bile	the
678	ostavi	leave
679	zadnja /e /i	last, rear, rearward, hinder, latest, hidden
680	ispred	in front, before, ahead of
681	nastavi	teaching
682	ceka, cekaju	waiting
683	svakako	surely, of course
684	dali	whether
685	onog	that
686	tražio	sought
687	prva	first
688	odgovor	the answer
689	kraja	end, in the end
690	traži	search, hark, tally-ho
691	mjesec, mjeseca, mjeseci	month, moon
692	svojoj	mine, his, to his
693	ucini	do, do it, make, render
694	vecer	evening, nightfall
695	ovih	of these
696	bofl	shoddy goods
697	cijelu	full
698	iako	although
699	curi	leaking
700	otišla	gone
701	postoje	exist, since
702	tvom	your
703	zbilja	really, stinging
704	naši /u /ih /im /oj	our, us, ourselves
705	tipa	type, make, mold
706	slušajte	listen up
707	potrebno	necessary, required
708	sastanak	meeting, date, rendezvous
709	drugu	another
710	telefon	telephone
711	shvacam	I understand
712	izaci	get out, go out, come out, exit
713	tih	quiet, stealthy, peaceful, placid
714	ondje	there

715	zbogom	goodbye
716	uci	enter, learn, teaches
717	poslao	sent out
718	pomozi	help
719	sestra /e /o /u	sister
720	govoriti	he speaks, speak
721	piše	it says
722	trebaju	they need, is necessary
723	jesmo	we are
724	shvatio	he realized
725	momak	guy
726	niko	no one
727	medu	honey, mead
728	hajdemo	Let's go, let's get
729	poziv	call, summons, invoke
730	tvojim	your, yours
731	druga	second, another
732	stavi	put, place
733	zemlje	buns
734	doktor	doctor
735	izvini	sorry, excuse me,
736	sretna /i /o	happy
737	red	order, progression, queue
738	noge	legs
739	zaboravio	forgot
740	poslu	business
741	vijesti	news
742	oce	father, fathers
743	znali	know
744	vidjet	to see
745	poznajem	I know
746	uraditi	to do
747	odvesti	always
748	prilika /u	quite
749	vjeruj	trust
750	kriv, krivim	guilty
751	stan /a /i /u /ica /ice /ite /je /ju	apartment, place, flat, home
752	svijeta	of the world
753	ubojica	the killer
754	brojiti	count
755	odlazi	leaves, go away, delay
756	tjedna	weeks
757	ubit	killed
758	poceo	started, began, commenced
759	uspio	successful
760	sobom	himself
761	eto	this
762	glavni	main, chief, major, key
763	obicno	usually
764	grada	town
765	krevet /u	bed

766	dolaze	they come
767	požuri	hurry up
768	jedva	barely, hardly, scarcely
769	spasiti	to save, to rescue
770	kralj /a	king
771	savršeno	thoroughly, perfectly
772	muž	husband
773	napad	attack
774	pustiti	let, allow
775	pokazati	show, demonstrate, display
776	svakog /a	every
777	igrati	to play
778	pas	dog
779	izlazi	exits
780	prokletstvo	damn it, perdition
781	kažete	tell
782	mici, micite	move
783	pravila	regulations, rules, technical specs
784	inace	otherwise
785	drugom	another
786	znak	sign
787	strašno	passionate, affectionate, -ly
788	gosp	Mr.
789	vraga	the devil
790	spremna	ready, prepared
791	veceru	dinner, supper
792	osjecaš	you feel
793	smisla	sense
794	pustite	leave, allow
795	gdo	Mrs.
796	pokušaj	attempt
797	pasaj	passage, corridor, mall, access
798	osjecaj	feeling, sentience
799	nemoguce	impossible
800	dešava	events, happens, happenings
801	dolazim	coming
802	idu	they go
803	prošlo	passed
804	postao	became
805	toj	the, he
806	brati	gather, pick, collect
807	dodite	come
808	škola, /e /i /o	school, academy, schools
809	strani	aside, extraneous
810	jutros	this morning
811	loš	bad
812	tvojoj	your, yours
813	srediti	arrange
814	zaustaviti	to stop, halt, block, stall, trap
815	hocemo	we will, we want, we wish
816	dobili	get

817	nova /u		new
818	zatvor		prison
819	izvinite		excuse me, pardon me
820	smijem		I can
821	cekati		to wait
822	osobno		personally
823	voljela		loved, liked
824	spusti		put it down, drop it
825	um		the mind, intellect, wit
826	srece		luck, chance
827	kapetan /a /e		captain
828	završiti		to complete
829	nove		new
830	njen /a		her
831	vašeg		your
832	šefe		safe
833	bica /e /u		being, creature, animal
834	umjesto		instead, in place of
835	dat		given, promised
836	jucer		yesterday
837	koristi /e /io /iti		use, utilise, used
838	izvuci		pull it out, extract, derive
839	sedam		seven
840	prestati		cease, quit, desist, depart
841	željela		wanted
842	zabavno		fun, entertainment, party
843	tice		concerns, concerning
844	zauvijek		forever
845	kunem		I swear
846	prošli		past, historic
847	imena		names
848	ajde!		Come on!
849	vjeruješ		you believe
850	nevjerojatno		incredibly
851	zatvoru		prison
852	vracam		I'm coming back
853	šteta		a pity, too bad
854	zoveš		call
855	veliku		great
856	nosi		bears
857	nazvati		called, named, nominated
858	ovuda		this way
859	posebno		especially
860	javi		answer
861	kuda		where
862	vodu		water
863	leda, led	ice	ice, icicles
864	glave		heads
865	ocito		obviously
866	hrana /u		food
867	postati		to become

868	stigao	arrived, catch up
869	trebate	you need
870	usta	mouth
871	dom	home
872	onoga	what, of that
873	mozak	brain
874	spavati	sleep, to sleep
875	krene /i	starts
876	pricam	witnesses
877	napravila /i	done, work, incur
878	sekunde /i /u	seconds
879	šef	safe, strongbox
880	budu	are
881	platiti	to pay, to defray
882	odeš	you leave
883	roditelji	parents
884	iznutr	inside
885	društvo	society, association
886	poceti	to begin
887	vratit	return
888	upoznao	get to know
889	glas	the voice, vote, sound, report, phone
890	cast /i	honor
891	cesto	often
892	vole	they like, they will, love
893	brinuti se	worry about, care for, be responble for
894	zemlja	gum, *zemlija* songs, volume
895	cura	girlfriend
896	kojim /a	by which
897	rukama	hands
898	izbora	of the election
899	godinama	for years
900	dala	provided
901	gospodin	Mister
902	ulazi	enter
903	kcer	daughter
904	ubili	killed
905	govorio	speaking
906	milijuna, miljun, miliona	million
907	izgubiti	to lose
908	kola	car
909	otišli	gone, go off, get over
910	knjiga /e /u	the book, book, a book
911	price	stories, narratives
912	kljuc	key, tool, wrench
913	jesti	eat
914	iznad	above
915	vrsta /e /u	species, type, kind, variety
916	promijeniti	to change, transmogrify
917	svakom	each, seamstress
918	razgovor /a	conversation

919	dopustiti	allow, permit, tolerate
920	nemate	you are not here
921	takva /e	such a, such, these
922	dogodi	happens
923	konacno	finally
924	kakvo	which
925	tražiti	look for, to seek
926	agent /a /e	agent, one working on behalf of another
927	slika /e /u	picture, pictures
928	budemo	we
929	zvati	call
930	išta	any
931	morala, morali	morals
932	dobila	got it
933	dvojica	two
934	pocinje	burst
935	rodendan	birthday
936	završio	done, finished, completed
937	uslugu	service, favor, accommodation
938	sljedeci	following
939	pošto	how much, since
940	ucinila	make, render, perform
941	ubojstvo	murder
942	onih	those
943	bježi	run, escape, evade
944	išao	went
945	drugim	others
946	zovu	they call
947	vratim	I return
948	kasnim	I'm late, *kasni*, delayed *kasno*, late
949	policajac	police officer
950	saznati	find out
951	gledao	watched
952	iskreno	sincerely, frankly, bluntly
953	shvatiti	realized, grasped
954	nestao	disappear
955	zovi	call
956	proci	go
957	novo /og /om	new
958	osam	eight
959	bitno	essentially
960	brodu	board
961	posljednja /e /i /o /u	last
962	odem	I'm going
963	upoznati	to meet, get to know
964	gdice	Miss
965	kladim	bet, wager
966	muškarac	a man
967	sjedni	sit down
968	riješiti	to solve, untangle, resolve
969	makni, maknite, maknuti	remove

970	cekam	I am waiting
971	udi	limbs
972	umrla	died
973	glavi	head
974	rado	I'm glad, gladly
975	pokušati to	attempt, to give it a try
976	kupi, kupiti	buy
977	našlu	headlines
978	drugih	other, others
979	pronašao	found
980	stranu	sides
981	tijela	bodies
982	pogledati	looked
983	onu	one
984	gle	Lo! (exclamation), look,
985	buduci, buducinost	future, *buducil da*, since, seeing as,
986	pokaži	show, demonstrate, display
987	zatim	then
988	nekad	once
989	zaboraviti	forget, abandon
990	pukovnice	Colonel
991	trenutno	currently, instantly, in the moment
992	smeta	counts
993	stalo	care, care about
994	napravi	make
995	ode	he goes
996	cestitam	congratulations
997	okolo	around
998	svaku	any, everyone
999	poslati	to send, to dispatch
1000	naucio	learned, picked up, trained
1001	nemaju	have
1002	buciti	roar, make noise, shout
1003	pišem / pisma / pismo	letters
1004	postaje /u	becomes
1005	vratite	return
1006	daje /o /te	gives, give
1007	veliko	big
1008	jeli	is it
1009	pricao	told
1010	gledam	I'm looking, I see
1011	opusti	relax, loosen
1012	pretpostav	assumptions, default configuration,
1013	uništiti	destroy
1014	piva, pive, pivi, pivo, pivu	beer
1015	gledaš	you look, you see, you watch
1016	nedostaje	missing
1017	ured	office, as part of the work
1018	dupe	buttocks
1019	psa	dog
1020	božic	god, idol, *božica*, goddess

1021	njihov	theirs
1022	zadatak	task, assignment, possibly behind
1023	recimo	let's say, let's assume
1024	zakon	law, statute, bylaw, rule
1025	ucinili	done
1026	izvan	beyond, out of, besides, without
1027	stici	arrive, reach, shields
1028	pomognem	let's help
1029	najviše	most
1030	držati	keep
1031	vezu	connection, relationship
1032	nauciti	learn, acquire
1033	nad	over the
1034	baci, baciti	throw
1035	avion /a	airplane, *avionom*, by air, by airplane
1036	spasio	saved
1037	nastaviti	go on, keep moving, keep going
1038	izbor	choice, election, option, selection
1039	dogovor	agreement, treaty, apointment, arrangement
1040	kava /e /u	coffee
1041	obecavam	I promise
1042	sjedi	sitting
1043	kupio, kupila	bought
1044	drugacije	different
1045	prokleti	accursed
1046	nazvao	called
1047	covek /a /e /i /o /u	man
1048	vratimo	let's return, payback
1049	jaja	eggs
1050	djecak	boy
1051	ostatak	vestige, remainder
1052	greška /u	error, fallacy, mistake, wrong
1053	pobjeci	to escape
1054	pokušava	trying to
1055	pogled	view, respect, review
1056	objasniti	explain
1057	pronašli	discover/discovered
1058	napokon	finally
1059	trebat	you need
1060	loša	moose
1061	vašem	your, yours
1062	sav	whole, complete
1063	cure	girls
1064	nogu	leg
1065	ubijen	killed
1066	ustvari	actually
1067	nikome	anyone
1068	držite	hold, retain, keep up, repute
1069	živim	I live
1070	ionako	anyways, already
1071	njihove	their

1072	glava	head, headpiece, noggin,
1073	svejedno	anyway, all the same, no preference
1074	smije	he laughs
1075	boriti	struggle, *boriti se* struggle with
1076	voda	water
1077	gubi	losing
1078	ispricavam	apologize, apologizes, explains
1079	govore	mostly
1080	staviti	place, play, put
1081	tvojih	your, yours
1082	vrijedi	valid
1083	dokaz	proof
1084	dole	down
1085	donio	brought
1086	tražiš	you are looking for
1087	igru	game
1088	nositi	to wear
1089	svojih	of their own
1090	seks	sex
1091	brava /o	lock, latch, safeguard
1092	pricaj	narrate, tell the tale
1093	stavio	put, place, play
1094	gledajte	look, watch, watch out!
1095	informacija /e /u	information
1096	lakše	easier
1097	kul	cool
1098	probleme	problem
1099	smiješ	you laugh, you can
1100	otkad	since
1101	pogrešno	wrong, mistakenly, in error
1102	trenutku	instant, point, juncture
1103	obzira	regardless
1104	vecina	the majority, most
1105	cuvaj	take care
1106	ostale	other
1107	ravno	just exactly flat
1108	gospodaru	my Lord
1109	uradi	work / office
1110	strah	fear, dread, fright
1111	ubila	killed
1112	tražimo	we are looking for
1113	došlo	there
1114	ubij	kill, slay
1115	vozi	drive, ride
1116	balvan	beam
1117	uspjeti	to succeed
1118	šališ	jokes
1119	autu	car
1120	prošle	former, preceding, precedent
1121	završi	completed
1122	upoznali	met

1123	lepo	nicely
1124	idete	you go
1125	svemu	all, everything
1126	imat	will
1127	poznaješ	know
1128	vrag	devil
1129	duboko	deep, deeply, profoundly
1130	slažem	I agree
1131	ukrao	stolen
1132	prozor	window
1133	jutr	tomorrow
1134	pao	fell down
1135	odlucio	decided
1136	dobit	profit, gain, prize.
1137	eno	one
1138	slobodna /i /o	free, freedom, freed
1139	predsjednik	president, chairman
1140	ulici	street
1141	zanimljivo	interesting, *zanimlj* I'm sorry, *zanim* to the woman
1142	racun /a /alo	account, bill, reckoning
1143	ijudi	people, folk,
1144	vide	see, vision, aspect
1145	hrane	food, nourishment
1146	nazovi	call, name, nominate
1147	pri	at in on, near, over
1148	lijevo	left
1149	zabava /e /i /u	fun, entertainment, party
1150	slušati	listen
1151	kam	nowhere
1152	ženi	wife
1153	pitaj	ask
1154	odjednom	bump, all of a sudden
1155	pokret	movement, motion
1156	stoji	stands
1157	zrak	air
1158	ubojstva	murders
1159	nademo	we find
1160	slobodan	free
1161	onim	those
1162	trebati	need, be necessary
1163	tajna	secret, the secret, mystery
1164	izvoli	choose
1165	gospodice	Miss
1166	uspjeli /o	succeeded
1167	desno	right
1168	karte	maps, charts, tickets, cards
1169	svojom	his, of his
1170	definitivno	definitely
1171	zadržati	keep it, keep,
1172	ostao	remained
1173	zvala	called

1174	jezik	language
1175	uzmite	take it away
1176	žive	live
1177	signal	warning
1178	napisao	wrote
1179	pocetak	start, inception
1180	poklon	gift, offering, bounty
1181	razmišljao	he thought
1182	hladno	cold
1183	pomislio	he thought
1184	cist /i /o /u	clean
1185	cime	what, whereby
1186	metara	meter, meters
1187	stvarima	affair, objects
1188	pun /a /i /o	full, filled, complete
1189	probudi	wake up
1190	osiguranje	insurance
1191	prsten	a ring, finger ring
1192	prati	wash, clean
1193	pada	well, yes
1194	opasno	dangerously
1195	rucak	lunch
1196	prošao	passed
1197	konja /e	horses, knights (chess)
1198	zadovoljstvo	satisfaction, zadovoljstv pleasure,
1199	duh	spirit, ghost, wraith, soul
1200	izvolite	please
1201	shvacaš	you understand
1202	veceri	evenings, dinner, supper
1203	donijeti	to bring
1204	cuda /o	wonders, miracle
1205	muža	muse
1206	nekada	sometimes
1207	sunca /e	sun, of the sun
1208	cuj	look
1209	odemo	let's go
1210	primjer	example, instance, paragon
1211	slucajno	by accident, by chance
1212	potreban	required
1213	traže	seeking, looking, tracking
1214	glup /a /ane /i /o	stupid, silly, dense, unintelligent
1215	otvorite	open, to open
1216	provjeriti	test, verify
1217	slicno	similar, similarly
1218	doveo	brought
1219	ocigledno	obvious, obviously
1220	razgovarao	spoke, conversed
1221	nos	nose
1222	nastavite	go on, keep moving, keep going
1223	potrebna	necessary, required
1224	nikakve	any

1225	sasvim	totally, completely, dead
1226	pametan /na /no	smart, clever, wise
1227	svatko	everyone
1228	donesi	bring, fetch, carry, retrieve
1229	njihova	their
1230	ocima	eyes
1231	korak	step, footstep
1232	odgovara	fit
1233	isuse	dry up, dessicate
1234	užasno	terribly
1235	nalazi	findings
1236	veza	connection, bond, link
1237	itko	anybody
1238	mesto	place
1239	ka	to, towards, onto, unto
1240	ušao	entered, came in
1241	govorite	speak
1242	opasnosti	dangers
1243	sustav	system
1244	zlato	gold
1245	iznenadenje	surprise
1246	trag	trail, clue, track
1247	dobrodošli	welcome
1248	vratila	brought back
1249	zaboga	earth, slang: for God's sake
1250	ubije	kill, kills
1251	srecu	chance
1252	narednice	will order, will instruct
1253	covece	man
1254	prekini /ite /u /uti	stop, interrupt
1255	vojska /e /u	army
1256	beba /e /u	doll, baby
1257	svoja	their own
1258	davno	long ago, of yore
1259	apsolutan	absolute, apsolutno, absolutely
1260	glad	hunger
1261	vašim	your, yours
1262	mirno	calmly
1263	pocela	started, begun
1264	prekasno	too late
1265	ostavila	left
1266	pomozite	help
1267	vragu	devil
1268	gleda	watching
1269	pomogao	helped
1270	niz	nobody
1271	usput	incidentally, by the way
1272	obojica	both
1273	verujem	I believe, trust
1274	bolestan	ill, sick,
1275	vlada /e	government

1276	pobjegao	runaway
1277	ženom	wife
1278	prijevod	translation
1279	prijateljica	friend, girlfriend
1280	doba	time, age, date, period
1281	provjeri	review
1282	pali	failed
1283	svjetlo	light, lights
1284	nicega	nothing
1285	sjajan	great, brilliant, gorgeous
1286	poci	burst, bursts
1287	svu	all, whole, complete
1288	narod	people
1289	fino	fine, finely, exquisite
1290	zacepi	shut, shut up
1291	dajem	I give
1292	cipele	shoes
1293	pobrinuti	take care
1294	takvo	such
1295	onako	so, like that, anyway
1296	mišljenje	opinion, view, thinking
1297	nikako	no way
1298	pozvao	invited, called
1299	razgovarali	talked
1300	sumnjam	I doubt, mistrust, distrust
1301	umre	he dies, passes away
1302	krivi, krivo, krivu	wrong
1303	podatke	data
1304	uzet	taken
1305	upomoc	help!
1306	lagao	lied
1307	devet	nine
1308	samnom	with me
1309	gdine	Mr.
1310	odlazim	I'm leaving, going go along
1311	živa	mercury, alive, quick, quicksilver
1312	uradim	I do
1313	stol	table
1314	dar	gift, offering, possibly talent
1315	živio	lived
1316	pažljivo	carefully
1317	zaustavi	stop it, *zausta* has really
1318	boja /e /i	color
1319	zlo	evil
1320	smece	trash, refuse
1321	pricekaj /jte /kati	hold on, wait
1322	budala	fool, idiot
1323	pomaže	helps
1324	pazite	watch your step
1325	pucaj	shoot
1326	spava	sleeping, he sleeps

1327	otkud	from where
1328	tacno	exactly, accurately
1329	posle	after
1330	tisuca	thousand
1331	nevolji	distress
1332	tiho	quietly
1333	okreni	hardened, cumbersome
1334	obecao	promised
1335	udario	hit, bump, strike
1336	ruka /e /u	hand, hands
1337	izasao	went out
1338	oduvijek	always
1339	udite	enter, hurt
1340	decka	boy
1341	svuda	everywhere
1342	glupost /i	nonsense
1343	razmisli	think, reflect
1344	vise	more, longer
1345	dam	give away
1346	šansu	chances
1347	poceli /o	started
1348	izgledam	I look
1349	normalno	normally
1350	pakao	hell
1351	zamisliti	imagine, think, conceive
1352	probaj /aji	try, try it
1353	odlican	excellent, cool, formidable!, fancy
1354	onom	that
1355	uglavnom	mainly, mostly
1356	ostane	stay
1357	nada /e /i	hope
1358	pozvati	to call, to ask, to invite
1359	ldemo	Let's go
1360	porucnice	Lieutenant
1361	komad	piece, chuck, shred, snippet
1362	ples	dance
1363	svjetla	light, lights
1364	pomalo	a little bit
1365	voziti	riding, commuting
1366	muškarci	men
1367	vratiš	return
1368	slatko	sweetly
1369	stiže	shields, coming
1370	dovesti	bring
1371	otkriti	to discover
1372	pristup	access
1373	kosu	hair
1374	zvijezda	star
1375	ostaje	continue, remain
1376	pobijediti	to win
1377	budete	you

1378	metak	bullet
1379	cule	bundles
1380	umire	dies, dying
1381	vratili	returned
1382	duže	longer, big
1383	mlada	bride
1384	blizina /i /u	nearness
1385	bojiš	scared
1386	voditi	to lead, to guide
1387	uhvatiti	catch
1388	potrebe	needs
1389	tišina	as a
1390	pitaš	you asked
1391	lov, lova, lovu	hunting
1392	težak	difficult, hard, trying, heavy, hefty
1393	dodem	I'm coming
1394	trci	run, is running, race
1395	živiš	live, possibly "fish"
1396	kaži	say
1397	gladan / gladna	hungry
1398	priznati	to admit
1399	sistem	model, chain, system
1400	odmor	rest
1401	držim	I'm holding
1402	vašoj	your
1403	doktora	doctorate
1404	izvuka	she pulled
1405	lmam	I have
1406	prijateljima	friends
1407	divan	nifty, superb
1408	vlak	train
1409	nocas	tonight
1410	veci	bigger, larger
1411	igre	games
1412	klinac	kid
1413	žrtva	victim
1414	šala	hall, auditorium
1415	dodeš	invite yourself over, you come
1416	smjesta	immediately
1417	poslali	sent, submitted, turned in
1418	pomogne	help, avail, assist
1419	krenuo, krenuli	started
1420	obaviti	carry out, to do
1421	rekoh	I said
1422	pripada	belongs to, relates to
1423	zid	wall, possibly Jew
1424	nož	knife, slice
1425	zatvori	close
1426	zvali	call
1427	tražili	sought
1428	uzeli	took, takeaway

1429	grozno	terrible, ghastly
1430	let	flight
1431	pažnja /e /i /o /u	attention
1432	nazvat	to call
1433	skroz	through, radically
1434	vjeruje	believes
1435	dobijem	I'll get it
1436	vraca	return, returns, coming back
1437	nigdje	nowhere
1438	nestala /e /i /o /u	disappeared, missing
1439	brine	worries
1440	savjet	advice, counsel, tip
1441	pojesti	consume
1442	umukni	shut up
1443	ocekivao	expected
1444	ocu	father, old man
1445	kompa	pal, friend, comrade
1446	popricati	talk, have a talk
1447	napustio /titi	left [a place], leave, abandon, forsake
1448	odjecu	clothing
1449	žrtve	victims
1450	most	bridge
1451	upoznala	met, inform
1452	pricamo	talk
1453	životinje	animals
1454	prvog	the first
1455	mlad, mladi	young, new, infant, child
1456	tajnu	secret, confidential
1457	pošteno	honestly, fair, fair enough
1458	spavao	slept
1459	usred	in the middle
1460	sreca	happiness, joy
1461	trudna	pregnant, expectant
1462	šuti	shut up, be silent
1463	kamion	truck
1464	tajne	secrets
1465	izlaz	exit
1466	najmanje	at least
1467	ulice	streets, to his face
1468	napada	attacks
1469	važi	okay, valid
1470	troje	three
1471	ljut, ljuta, ljuti	angry, bitter, cross
1472	tjedana	weekly
1473	udarac	impact, blow, striker
1474	velik	large, big
1475	tad	then
1476	izgledaju	look, seem, or appear
1477	karta /u	map, chart, ticket, card
1478	de	give
1479	ozbiljan	serious, grave, severe

1480	vjerovao	believed
1481	najveca /e /i	largest
1482	dvoji	doubts
1483	kriste	Christ
1484	nažalost	unfortunately
1485	njene /og /om /u	its
1486	stati	what do you..., Stop
1487	malog, malom	a little bit, small
1488	tijekom	during
1489	kceri	daughters
1490	brak	marriage, matrimony, wedding
1491	pitala	she asked
1492	drugoj	another
1493	vodim	I lead
1494	receno	told
1495	pokušavaš	trying
1496	totalno	totally
1497	ej	Hey, hallo!
1498	sud	Court, tribunal, vessel, judiciary
1499	popraviti	fix, repair, mend
1500	unutar	within, inside
1501	tražite	looking for
1502	valja	cylinder
1503	razumijete	you understand
1504	sjednite	seat
1505	seksi	sexy
1506	ugovor	contract
1507	gda	Ms.
1508	vatru	fire, light, the passion
1509	zamisli	ideas
1510	ubija	kills
1511	pokazat	show, demonstrate, display
1512	prošlost	yesteryear, foregone
1513	lijek	drug, narcotic, remedy
1514	željeli	like, zeljel our goal
1515	novine	newspaper
1516	dve	two
1517	razgovaramo	we talk, we parlay
1518	vijest	news
1519	otkrio	revealed, exposed
1520	zapovijed	command, *-je* commanded, *zapovi* frogs, *zapo* frog
1521	mislimo	we think
1522	taksi	cab, taxi
1523	prihvatiti	to accept
1524	obzirom	considering
1525	zatvora	prison
1526	cilj	goal, object, intent
1527	njezin	her
1528	klub	club
1529	odluka /e /u	decision, decisions
1530	uzela	took, takeaway

1531	iste	asks
1532	umoran	tired
1533	sjajna	great, resplendent
1534	bedem	wall, barricade, obstacle
1535	pita	pie
1536	pozdrav	greeting, salutation
1537	gospodar	Lord, liege, sovereign, dynast
1538	izvrsno	great, excellent
1539	izvještaj	report, notice, account
1540	kojom	which
1541	vikend	weekend
1542	engleski	English
1543	dušu	soul
1544	skupa	expensive
1545	stoga	therefore, stomach, so,
1546	zaveži	charming
1547	pokušala /e /i /o /u	tried, attempted
1548	kontakt	contact
1549	sinko	son, sonny
1550	nosiš	wear
1551	ustani	stand up
1552	obrada	processing
1553	skini	download, shed, take off
1554	vratima	the door, portal
1555	brinem	I worry
1556	more, moru	sea
1557	brisa	wipe, mop, erase, cleanse
1558	muškarca	man
1559	kamen	stone
1560	slušam	hello
1561	zlocina	crime
1562	kreten	moron
1563	platio	pay
1564	dužnost	duty, obligation, office, trust
1565	podnijeti	share, submit, endure
1566	saznao	found out
1567	podrucje /u	territory
1568	sudbina /u	fate, destiny, doom
1569	položaj	position, office, job
1570	mož	husband
1571	završili	completed
1572	povijest /i	history
1573	vjencanje	wedding
1574	ispricajte /ispricati	tell, narrate, relate
1575	odvjetnik	always
1576	nosim	wear
1577	napravim /s /t	do, make, cause
1578	tatu	thief
1579	pricali	testified
1580	kriva	curve
1581	obje	both

1582	pokušat	try
1583	droga /e /u	drug
1584	pravilo	norm, law, precept, ordinance, scripture
1585	laži, leži	lies
1586	obožavam	love, I adore
1587	velikog	great
1588	necega	something
1589	mesa, meso	meat, flesh, broth
1590	pucati	to shoot
1591	bore, bori	fight
1592	razgovaram	I'm talking
1593	zvuk	sound
1594	ceš	you'll
1595	odgovori	answers
1596	važan	important, serious, pertinent
1597	cijenim	appreciate
1598	promijenio	changed, altered
1599	stavite	put, play
1600	uhvati	caught, capture, grasp
1601	otkaz	notice
1602	takode	so that, also
1603	njime	it
1604	divna	beautiful, superb, lovely, adorable
1605	situaciju	circumstances
1606	povrijediti	hurt, to hurt
1607	verovatno	probable, likely
1608	šansa	a chance
1609	pripremite	preparation
1610	centar, centru	center
1611	napolje /u	out, outside
1612	ucinit	do, do it, make, render
1613	bomba	bomb, grenade, or shell; explosive
1614	pratiti	accompany, escort
1615	situacija	situation, the situation
1616	dokaze	prove, evidence
1617	životinja	animals
1618	pošalji	job, send, sends
1619	pokazao	showed, demonstrated
1620	vojnik	a soldier
1621	tražila	sought
1622	razumio	understood
1623	poludio	went crazy
1624	nacina	find on
1625	dozvoliti	allow, permit, license, authorize
1626	izvor	source, well, spring, derivation
1627	dozvolu	permit, license, permission
1628	iskren	sincere, genuine, candid
1629	deo	part, a part of, portion, share, piece
1630	dvaput	twice
1631	pol	gender
1632	zapamti	remember, memorize

1633	provesti	guide, show through
1634	caj	tea
1635	pustio	released
1636	djeluje	works
1637	razmišljam	I'm thinking
1638	vjerovatno	probably, likely
1639	velikim	big, large
1640	zaboravila	oblivion
1641	strana	country
1642	onome	what
1643	otprilike	about, roughly, approximately
1644	sacekaj	wait
1645	bolest	sickness, illness, disease
1646	svo	all, whole, complete
1647	dokaza	evidence
1648	rupa /e /u	hole, burrow, pit
1649	sredi	Wednesday, middle of
1650	pocetka /u	to begin
1651	ostala	the remainder, the rest
1652	prve	first
1653	takvu	such
1654	cekao	waited
1655	dokazati	prove it
1656	dug	debt, obligation
1657	proveo	spent, exhausted
1658	trenutka	moment, point, juncture
1659	preživjeti	survive, outlive
1660	citao, citati	read
1661	ovisi	depends
1662	smijemo	we can
1663	cekamo	we are waiting
1664	jak	stiff, strong, intense, solid
1665	dodu	come
1666	dorucak	breakfast
1667	oba / obe	both, either
1668	telefona	telephone
1669	njeno	hers
1670	dama /o /u	lady
1671	energije	energy
1672	kljuceve	keys
1673	zgrade	buildings
1674	mozga	brains
1675	ubijem	I kill
1676	djecaka	boys
1677	uradili	have done
1678	shvatila /i	realized, grasped
1679	vremenu	time
1680	lik	character
1681	meta	target
1682	neprijatelj	the enemy
1683	putovanje	the trip

1684	prokleto	cursed
1685	piti	drink
1686	uradila	did
1687	pamet	head, mind, brain, intellect
1688	daja	that I
1689	izdržati	to handle, resist, withstand,
1690	šalim	I'm kidding, joking
1691	svoga	his, of his
1692	treci	third, the third
1693	diraj	touch, feel, finger
1694	smirite	calm down
1695	zauzet	busy
1696	drugima	others
1697	podi	floor
1698	tajni	secret, undercover, furtive
1699	dogovoreno	deal
1700	uradiš	do it
1701	postane	becomes
1702	govor	speech, address, talk, discourse
1703	predivno	wonderful, wonderfully
1704	sredio	arrange
1705	javite /i	call, inform, notify
1706	starog	old
1707	roden	born
1708	hitno	urgently
1709	sjetiti	to remember
1710	odatle	from there
1711	milja	mile
1712	pukovnik	Colonel
1713	pokazuje	shows, demonstrate, displays
1714	zabrinut	worried
1715	opasnost	danger
1716	prošla	former, foregone
1717	curo /u	girl
1718	miris	smell
1719	coja	scarf
1720	drvo	wood
1721	ubiješ	kill
1722	grupa /e	groups, band, team(s), squad
1723	posve	completely, seem, quite
1724	pojavio	appeared
1725	brojan	numerous
1726	procitao	to read
1727	prodati	dispose of
1728	vece	the evening, larger, the night
1729	prvu	first
1730	nesreca /e /i /o /u	accident, accidents
1731	vojnice /i	soldier, soldiers
1732	operacija /e /u	operation, operations
1733	ruci	lunch
1734	vrat	neck

1735	nocu	at night, nightly
1736	stigla	pin, arrived
1737	adresa / u	address
1738	zahvaliti	thank
1739	savršen	perfect
1740	sigurnost	security
1741	cinjenica /i /o /u	fact
1742	dobiješ	you get it
1743	postala	became
1744	supruga	wife, spouse, lady
1745	gori	burning, worse
1746	zraka /u	air
1747	petak	Friday
1748	djevojcica	girls
1749	velicanstvo	splendor, majesty
1750	slijedeci	next, following
1751	muci	passion
1752	kraljica	queen
1753	popodne	afternoon
1754	kci	daughter
1755	tisuce	thousands
1756	opasan	dangerous
1757	žalim	I regret, rue, mourn, deplore, lament
1758	vojnika	soldiers
1759	neprijatelja	of the enemy
1760	dovedi	bring take lead
1761	volimo	we love
1762	vaših	your, yours
1763	kosa	hair
1764	poznato	known
1765	zlocin	crime
1766	djed, djeda	grandfather
1767	zla	evil
1768	sladak	sweet, sleek, cute
1769	dopusti´	leave, permit
1770	išla	go
1771	posvuda	everywhere
1772	iskoristiti	to use it, use, employ, utilize, make the most of
1773	jednostav	simple steps
1774	dobije	he gets it
1775	šerif	sheriff
1776	samog	himself
1777	nijedan	no, none, neither
1778	otkrili	reveal, disclose, expose
1779	razumjeti	you understand
1780	razumem	I understand
1781	nevolja /e	trouble, distress, teen
1782	traje	last, continue
1783	uhvatio	caught
1784	živjeli	cheers
1785	lma	there's

1786	krug	lap
1787	dami	that we
1788	nedavno	recently
1789	dovidenja	bye, goodbye, cheerio! - See also *Cao/Ciao*
1790	sjecate	you remember, you recall
1791	borba	battle, struggle, difficulty, *borbamil*, combat
1792	izade /i	out
1793	uhvatili	caught
1794	prošlosti	former, preceding
1795	cek	check
1796	laž, lagati	lie
1797	okej	okay
1798	bek	back
1799	lažeš	you're lying
1800	predsjednika	President, chairman, leader
1801	požurite	hurry, rush, hasten
1802	zube	teeth
1803	blag /o	mild, *blagost*, mildness, meekness
1804	sjesti	take a seat
1805	osjecao	felt
1806	tokom	during, throughout, in the course of
1807	igraš	games, you play
1808	ženama	women
1809	mrzi	he hates
1810	odgovornost	responsibility
1811	gadno	bad, nasty
1812	stariji	older, senior
1813	loptu	ball
1814	crven /a /e /i /o /u	red
1815	išli	switch, walk, go by
1816	snaga /e /u	force, strength, power
1817	plesati	dance
1818	pogodi	take a guess
1819	stroj	machines
1820	udari	strike, strikes
1821	ucinim	I do
1822	navecerin	the evening
1823	ekipa /u	team
1824	prokleta	cursing
1825	slušaš	you listen
1826	vruce	hot, very warm, possibly: I'm lying
1827	nek	some
1828	cuje	hears
1829	bacio	threw
1830	uzmem	take
1831	momce	boy
1832	osjeca	feels
1833	sumnje	suspicions, doubts
1834	uopšte	at all, general
1835	pijan	drunk, stoned, intoxicated
1836	ujak	uncle

91

1837	ukoliko if,		inasmuchas
1838	vau		wow, woof
1839	zgodan		convenient
1840	volite		he loves you
1841	nikog		anyone
1842	držiš		hold on, possibly wet
1843	jede /jedu		eat
1844	ponosan		proud
1845	dodatan		additional
1846	poslat		sent
1847	katkad		sometimes
1848	trik		trick, ruse, gimmick
1849	uradimo		Let's do it
1850	živimo		live
1851	visoko		highly
1852	zadrži		hold it, retain, detain, delay, reserve
1853	gospod		the LORD
1854	pogledam		glance, see, look
1855	spavanje		sleeping
1856	nabaviti		get [something], purchase, acquire
1857	dodavola		what the devil !?
1858	heroj		hero
1859	vino		wine
1860	pobijedio		won
1861	rak		cancer, crab
1862	pokažem		show, demonstrate, display
1863	krecemo		embarking, setting forth
1864	torbu		bag, pouch
1865	cudovište		monster, monsters
1866	poštovanje		respect, esteem
1867	drukcije		differently
1868	ubojice		killers
1869	umrijet		to die
1870	preuzeti		Take over, will take over
1871	poznajete		you know
1872	zaštititi		protect, defend, shield, screen, harbor
1873	oprostiti		forgive
1874	izvesti		perform, export, derive, bring out
1875	cina		act
1876	država		state, country
1877	govorimo		we speak
1878	pocne		it starts
1879	kutija, kutiju		box
1880	podataka		data, information
1881	voljeti		to love, to be fond of
1882	lijecnik, lijenika		doctor
1883	iduci		next, other
1884	ptica		bird
1885	hodati		walk
1886	razlika		difference
1887	vatra		fire, the light

1888	predati	deliver, to hand over, surrender
1889	mijenja	change, changing
1890	bora	wrinkle
1891	bivši	former, ex-, one-time
1892	popiti	drink, consume
1893	njihovu	their
1894	sprijeciti	prevent
1895	hlace	pants
1896	skinuti	remove, take down
1897	diži	hoist, rear, raise; also possibly sequence
1898	odavno	a long time ago
1899	dete	child
1900	ponašanje	behavior, conduct
1901	sjediti	to sit
1902	vlasnik	owner, proprietor
1903	pridružiti	join, to join
1904	stoja	stands
1905	dvojic	pairs
1906	cijelom	whole, complete, full
1907	kojih	which
1908	pomaz	annointing
1909	odgovoran	responsible
1910	otok /a /e /i /o /u	island
1911	pogriješio	wrong
1912	zadnjih	last, rear, rearward, hinder, latest, hidden
1913	uredaj	device, gadget, machine
1914	pozovi	call, invite, ask
1915	baka	grandmother
1916	pritisak	pressure
1917	slijedi	follows, coming up
1918	drv	firewood
1919	dolaziš	coming
1920	tvojom	your, yours
1921	planeta	planet
1922	riba /e /u	fish, fishes
1923	prodao	sold
1924	skloni	inclined, prone, remove
1925	novaca	money
1926	slobodu	freedom
1927	crtez	drawing, drafting
1928	laže	easier
1929	igrao	played
1930	pisati	to write
1931	daš	gives, give
1932	Americi, Amerika	The United States of America
1933	prode	passes, go through, pass by
1934	pacijent	patient
1935	dnevnik	diary, journal, planner
1936	odgovoriti	to answer
1937	konj	horse, knight (chess)
1938	voleo	like, loved, fond of

1939	poznat	known
1940	spoj	compound, joint, connection
1941	izgledati	look
1942	dosadno	boring
1943	americki	An American person
1944	ulaz	entrance, doorway
1945	svetu	world
1946	granice	borders
1947	svidaš	like you, you like it
1948	neznam	I do not know
1949	pogledao	looked
1950	predlažem	I suggest
1951	go	naked, nude, or bare
1952	sljedece	the following
1953	mobitel	cell phone
1954	dobrog	well-meaning, good intentioned, benevolent
1955	probati	to try, try out
1956	pravim	I make, I say
1957	želeo	I wanted to
1958	prvom	initial, leading
1959	vecera	dinner
1960	prekrasna, /o	too late
1961	pjesma a	song, songs, song
1962	sigurnosti	certitude
1963	cujemo	we hear
1964	vjetar	wind
1965	vozim	I am driving
1966	vodite	lead
1967	nadao	hoped
1968	pare	steam, money
1969	ocekujem	I expect
1970	briljant	brilliant, bright, shiny
1971	zovite	call
1972	sreo	meet
1973	banke /a /u	bank
1974	cvijece	flowers
1975	dugujem	I owe
1976	prst	finger, digit
1977	drže	hold on
1978	odlicna	excellent
1979	braca	brothers, brethren
1980	ostaneš	you stay
1981	necemu	to something
1982	odijelo	a suit, clothing, outfit
1983	pocni	start
1984	dužnosti	responsibility
1985	vjerujete	you believe
1986	selo	village, countryside
1987	nosio	wearing
1988	završila	completed
1989	spasi	save

1990	ponavljam	I repeat
1991	razliku	divergence
1992	najgore /i	worst
1993	vjerujte	trust
1994	uistinu	indeed, truly
1995	mrtvih	of the dead
1996	izabrao	he chose
1997	cista /e	cyst
1998	izabra	she chooses
1999	smrdi	smell, it stinks
2000	kosti	bone
2001	popis	drink, swallow
2002	pogodio /iti	affect, score, plug
2003	pozornost	attention
2004	nagrada /u	reward, award, prize, bounty, stake
2005	pokušavao	trying to
2006	svet	holy, the world
2007	citav	whole, complete, full
2008	restoran	restaurant, diner
2009	išl	and similar, etc.
2010	prodaju	sale
2011	duša	soul, spirit, psyche, fig. Inner tube, bladder
2012	pricala	told, narrated
2013	ponoviti	repeat
2014	miran	quiet
2015	clan	member
2016	gospoda	Mrs.
2017	odgovore	answers
2018	upali	turned on
2019	govorila	say, tell, speak, talk
2020	pucao	shot
2021	kratko	briefly
2022	trajati	last, continue
2023	zvijezde	stars
2024	zgradu	buildings
2025	stotine	hundred, hundreds
2026	pala	fell
2027	neba /e /o /u	the sky, heavens, heaven
2028	poslala	sent
2029	vatre	fire, light, the passion
2030	zapovjednik	commander, squadron,
2031	planove	design
2032	životom	life
2033	potez	movement, stroke, line
2034	oženjen	married
2035	vozila	vehicles
2036	zaboravite	forget it!
2037	ciniti	do
2038	poseban	special, distinct,
2039	ostanem	I stay
2040	postaviti	set up

2041	uvjeriti	to persuade, to convince
2042	bas	bass, basso
2043	sreli	met
2044	svemir /u	universe, space
2045	stajati	stand
2046	polja /e /i /o /u	fields / field
2047	velikom	huge, great
2048	zakona	law, statute, principle, regulation
2049	placa	salary
2050	napao	attacked
2051	poznaje	know
2052	osjecati	feel
2053	krece	moves, moving
2054	nekakav	some, any
2055	gdica	Miss
2056	odavdje	from here
2057	spavala	slept
2058	slatka	sweet, sleek, cute
2059	nadeš	you find
2060	ocem	eyes
2061	završim	completed, i'm sorry
2062	videti	see
2063	odustati	give up, quit, lay off
2064	sredit	arranged
2065	nalog	order, warrant, command
2066	davola	devil
2067	odrastao	grown up, fully grown, adult
2068	uništio	destroyed, destroyed by
2069	ucinite	do it
2070	pronašla	found
2071	spomenuo	mentioned
2072	ukljucujuci	including, inclusive
2073	osiguranja	insurance
2074	misija, misiju	missions, mission
2075	vodio	led
2076	stolu	stole
2077	napasti	attack, invade, jump, offend
2078	odlucili	decided
2079	pogodak	hit, shot
2080	šalje	sending
2081	uspjela	succeed
2082	probudio	woke up
2083	dobrodošao	welcome
2084	ispravno	brutally
2085	ubijena	killed, slayed
2086	gubitak	loss
2087	ubrzo	soon, before long
2088	budalo	you fool
2089	zaljubljen	in love, *zaljub, zaljublj* fall in love
2090	izgledao	looked
2091	sudu	dishes

2092	kiša	rain
2093	prolazi	pass, passage
2094	zaustavite	shut down
2095	bolesna /nik	patient, one undergoing treatment
2096	igram	I'm playing
2097	visosti	height, highness
2098	djelo	work
2099	dopustite	allow, permit, tolerate
2100	tragove	traces
2101	opa	oops, wow, oh well
2102	teška	heavy, serious, weighty
2103	opremu	equipment
2104	crn /a /e /i /o /u	black
2105	odjel	department, section, bureau
2106	vozilo	vehicle
2107	poljubac	kiss
2108	nasamoin	private, discreetly
2109	držao	kept, held, support, wield
2110	odvedi	always
2111	osecam	I feel
2112	izgledate	you look
2113	svjedoka	witnesses
2114	glavom	head, headpiece, noggin,
2115	dodaj	add
2116	pripremi	prepare, make ready
2117	bos	barefooted
2118	pušku	gun
2119	krenemo, krenite, krenuti	go
2120	ulica	street, block
2121	sazna	finds out, learn
2122	dosad	by far, hitherto
2123	autobus	bus, omnibus
2124	istom	the same
2125	vina	wine
2126	otvorena /e /i /o /u	poisonous
2127	raj	paradise, eden
2128	posjetiti	to visit
2129	novinama	newspapers
2130	duga	rainbow, debt
2131	jedni	each
2132	završimo	completed, admiration, we are feeling good.
2133	pasti	collapse
2134	obzir	consideration, regard, respect, view
2135	devojka / e	girl, girls
2136	sigurnom	secure, safe
2137	igramo	play, dance, perform
2138	igri	game
2139	cine	make
2140	cuvati, cuvar	guard
2141	prolaz	passage, aisle, gateway, breach
2142	propustio	missed, omission, oversight

2143	tisucu	a thousand
2144	roditelja /e	parents
2145	paziti	pay attention, beware
2146	nogama	off
2147	pokušavaju	try, attempt
2148	gledaju	watch, watch out, look out, observe
2149	ciniš	you do
2150	videla	see, saw
2151	važna	important, seriously
2152	hitnu	Emergency, *hitn* emergency room
2153	ljudska, ljudski, ljudsko	human
2154	pokušavamo	trying to
2155	iznutra	from the inside
2156	primljeno	received
2157	dine	dunes
2158	prodaje	selling, sales
2159	sveta	world
2160	straha	fear, fears
2161	izvukao	out, tug, draw out
2162	razmišljati	ruminate, meditate
2163	vjeruju	they believe
2164	stvorio	create, produce, beget
2165	podigni	pick up, lift up
2166	tima	team
2167	bijel /i	white, blank
2168	sveto	holy
2169	pobrini	take care
2170	desi	where are you,
2171	udar	strike, stroke, impact
2172	smisao	meaning
2173	spavam	I'm sleeping
2174	uzmeš	take, pick up
2175	tren	instant
2176	jedi	dishes, meals
2177	neobicno	unusual
2178	fer	fair,
2179	jeo	eating
2180	poginuo	killed, perish, perished
2181	odlucila	decided
2182	poznavao	knew
2183	spremno	ready
2184	države	States, countries
2185	meduvremenu	meanwhile, *meduvreme* split time
2186	zahvaljujuci	thanks to, with the help of, by virtue of, *zahvalju* my gratitude
2187	kat	floor
2188	predstavlja	represents
2189	uši	ears
2190	ovakav	like this, this kind of
2191	odveo	always
2192	poziva	call, summons, invoke
2193	vrhu	tip, summit, point

2194	pravom	real, right, straight
2195	jace	more, stronger
2196	dogovorili	agreed
2197	pricate	talking
2198	umrem	I will die
2199	linija, liniji, liniju	line, *linije* lines
2200	padne	will fall, collapse, fall down
2201	pojavi	appears
2202	ocekuje	expects
2203	zamisao	idea, imagine, imagination
2204	lmaš	you've got
2205	gledala	watching
2206	neugodno	unpleasantly
2207	ušli	leaked
2208	postojati	exist, to respect
2209	braku	pertaining to marriage, bridal, matrimonial
2210	sveti	saint
2211	šešir	a hat
2212	gade	bastard
2213	kažemo	we say
2214	iskustva	experiences
2215	umu	mind, wit, intellect
2216	priuštiti	afford
2217	prostor	room, space, scope
2218	osjetiti	sense, experience
2219	ciji	whose
2220	zatvoriti	close, shut, shut off
2221	mrdaj	move
2222	vještica	witch
2223	nazvala	called, named, nominated
2224	pricaju	talking
2225	porucnik	Lieutenant
2226	šefa	safe deposit box
2227	primio	to receive
2228	zgrada	building
2229	porodica /e /i /o /u	family, relatives
2230	promjena	changing, transition, declension
2231	ponudu	offer
2232	cvrsta /e /i /o /u	firm, firmly
2233	drugdje	elsewhere
2234	krasno	neatly
2235	uciniš	do, make, render
2236	spavaš	you sleep
2237	natjerati	make, compel, drive, force
2238	odluciti	decided, decreed, ordained
2239	leti	years
2240	odete	you go, go away
2241	razgovarat	to talk
2242	znanje	knowledge
2243	njihovim	theirs
2244	tomu	also, in addition

2245	letjeti	fly
2246	povratak	return, recovery
2247	tvrdi	claims, solid, firm
2248	hvala	Thanks
2249	riskirati	to take a risk
2250	raste	growing
2251	predsjednice	President
2252	svidjeti	please, suit
2253	ulogu	role, stake, bet
2254	javit	I'll
2255	kaznu	penalty
2256	ustaj	mouth
2257	psi	canine
2258	vremenom	temporarily
2259	prestao	stopped
2260	jaka /e	great, strong, powerful
2261	fantasticno	fantastic
2262	pokupiti	pick up, lift up
2263	smio	dared
2264	koljena	knee, *koljen* elbow
2265	gubimo	losing
2266	javio	reported, informed
2267	ptice	birds
2268	poslom	business, transaction
2269	pucajte	plug
2270	povuci	withdraw, to pull, to pull back
2271	vrijedno	valuable
2272	plana	plan
2273	novcem	money
2274	glavna	main, primary, principal
2275	gledali	watch
2276	iskustvo	experience
2277	odlazimo	leaving
2278	vracamo	we return
2279	bogom	God
2280	krivica	fault
2281	jedinice	units
2282	zovete	calling
2283	oružjem	weapons
2284	dozvoli	permit, permitting
2285	obican	plain
2286	promjene	changes, alters, transforms
2287	normalan	normal, regular
2288	njezina	hers
2289	haljinu	robes, dresses, clothes, gown
2290	cekaš	waiting for
2291	desiti	where are you,
2292	naroda /e	nations
2293	stoje	what is it?
2294	zvat	beckon
2295	spustite	release, put down

2296	zaštitu	protection, patronage, aegis, care, safeguard
2297	sudac	referee
2298	dvadeset	twenty
2299	glazba /u	music, see also muzika
2300	probuditi	to awaken
2301	djeteta	child
2302	energiju	energy
2303	dopada	like, likes
2304	razmišljaš	you think
2305	pozdravi	greeting
2306	rješenje	solution, settlement
2307	drugoga	another
2308	bazu	base
2309	svašta	everything
2310	uspori	slow down
2311	kolima	car
2312	ulicu	street
2313	procitati	to read
2314	proklet	curse
2315	umiru	in peace, at rest
2316	grudi	chest, bosom
2317	zovemo	call
2318	poslove	affairs, jobs
2319	hod	throw, cast, pitch
2320	namjerno	deliberately
2321	plaši	scares
2322	prijem	entrance, reception
2323	vozio	driving, commuting
2324	duha	spirit, ghost, wraith, soul
2325	zaslužio	deserved, earned,
2326	rezultat	the result
2327	umorna	tired
2328	noga	foot, leg
2329	gaz	beam (width of ship), wade
2330	policajci	police officers
2331	šumi	amount, sum, total
2332	napisati	write
2333	duguješ	you owe, you owe it
2334	velikoj	great, huge
2335	rijeke	rivers
2336	bojati	to fear, *bojati se*, to be afraid of
2337	ociju	eyes
2338	nervozan	nervous
2339	kreveta	beds
2340	osloboditi	release, relieve, deliver
2341	udati	marry, to marry, to give in marriage
2342	oluja	storm, tempest
2343	para	fumes, damp, vapor
2344	izgledalo	looked
2345	cvrst	sturdy
2346	smijete	you may, must

2347	predugo	too long
2348	sakriti	to hide, conceal
2349	zaslužuje	deserves
2350	princ	Prince
2351	rukom	by hand
2352	makar	at least
2353	del	part
2354	donijela	brought
2355	boru	boron
2356	umirem	dying, I am dying
2357	njihovo	their
2358	nedelje	weeks
2359	Isus	Jesus
2360	kombi	van, panel truck
2361	jelo	dish, eating, serving
2362	teže	thesis, more difficult, weight
2363	narednik	Sergeant
2364	kap	drop, stroke
2365	provjerio	checked
2366	sinu	son
2367	ude	limbs
2368	katu	floor, story, level
2369	pošaljite	send, sends
2370	uzimam	I take
2371	znaciti	mean
2372	dosje	dossier
2373	ucinimo	do, let's do it
2374	pica	pizza
2375	budan	awake
2376	gad	cad, scoundrel
2377	cijena /e /i /o /u	price
2378	utakmicu	match, game
2379	primiti	accept, admit, receive
2380	drugaciji	different
2381	nimalo	not at all
2382	postali	become, originate
2383	služi	serves, service
2384	izraz	expression, figure of speech
2385	primijetio	figure, character, image
2386	samoubojstvo	suicide
2387	hrabrosti	courage
2388	ceo	all
2389	oblik	form
2390	ovakve	thus, in this way
2391	prijevoz	transport, cargo
2392	zezaš	Jazz, *Zeza* the scepter, *zez* cross, *ze* that
2393	jedinica	unit, integer, one
2394	sise	breasts
2395	otkako	since when
2396	druže	dude, Comrade
2397	amerikanci	An American person

2398	ubiju	they kill
2399	poljubi	kiss
2400	stao	stopped
2401	predstavu	idea, show, performance
2402	kukavica	coward
2403	pametni	smart phone
2404	mrtvog	dead
2405	htela /htjela /i /htjeti	wanted
2406	uživaj	enjoy, savor, relish
2407	ugodan	nice, delightful, pleasant
2408	stavile	exhibition
2409	papir	paper
2410	nastavimo	continuing, let's continue, teaching
2411	pratio	followed
2412	ajmo	let's
2413	sjetio	remembered
2414	problemi	problems
2415	uzorak	sample, pattern, model
2416	prste	fingers
2417	onima	he has
2418	odnos	relationship, ratio, bearing
2419	ugodno	comfortable, nice
2420	helikopter	helicopter
2421	crpsti	to pump, draw out
2422	policajca	a police officer
2423	ureda	office
2424	osjecaje	feelings
2425	platit	pay
2426	objašnjenje	explanation
2427	službeno	officially
2428	svidaju	like them, they like it
2429	udara	shock, strike, pound
2430	sanjao	dreamed
2431	navodno	allegedly
2432	novim	new
2433	nikakvog	no, none
2434	jednako	equally
2435	detektive	detective
2436	štogod	Whatever, what?
2437	pokraj	beside, along, by
2438	jadni	poor, miserable, wretched
2439	voljeli	loved, liked
2440	djecom	children
2441	nikakavno,	poor, needy
2442	suviše	too
2443	zgradi	buildings
2444	vozac	driver, motorist
2445	pojeo	eat
2446	prošlog	preceding
2447	planine	mountains
2448	želja	wish, zelija cell

2449	ubojicu	killer
2450	svjedok	witness, onlooker, deponent
2451	zamalo	almost, *zama* for me
2452	sok	juice
2453	ugasi	turn off
2454	nose	wear
2455	pijem	I drink
2456	molimo, moli	pray, ask, request
2457	bogovi	the gods
2458	nov	new
2459	roditeljima	parents
2460	pogoden	weather
2461	zahvalan	thankful, thank you, grateful
2462	donijet	bring
2463	pomogneš	help
2464	savršena	consumate
2465	pozvala	invited, called, asked
2466	izbaciti	kick out, eject, jettison, dispose, delete, cut out
2467	barut	gunpowder
2468	krov	roof
2469	pocnemo	let's start
2470	dvojicu	two
2471	pluca	lungs, lights
2472	kis	vinegar
2473	odlazite	go away
2474	direktno	directly
2475	povesti	take, bring
2476	svidjelo	liked it
2477	slucaja	contingency, instance
2478	vojsci	army
2479	brzinu	speed
2480	suprug	husband, spouse, mate
2481	macka	cat
2482	kontrolirati /om /u	control, controller, monitor, checkpoint
2483	prednost	advantage
2484	bojao	feared
2485	cijelog	around, about, close to
2486	rani, rano	early
2487	tužno	sad
2488	prijateljice	friends
2489	obecajem	I promise
2490	smiju	they may
2491	poslušaj	listen
2492	jedem	I eat
2493	pratite	accompany, escort
2494	uzrok	cause
2495	cašu	time
2496	oprezan	careful, cautious, deliberate
2497	grud	clumps
2498	dovodi	brings, drives
2499	slomio	broke, crush, fracture

2500	osjetio	felt
2501	rizik	risk
2502	razmisliti	to think
2503	gledate	you're watching
2504	završava	ends
2505	hrabrost	bravery
2506	dijela	part
2507	takvim	such
2508	muda	mud
2509	nebi	not
2510	preživio	the living, survivors, survive
2511	podu	the floor, the lowest level, the bottom
2512	bocu	bottle
2513	dolazimo	we are coming, we come
2514	uzme	take
2515	uživo	live
2516	zahtjev	claim, request,
2517	smjeru	direction
2518	lici	cheeks
2519	kuhinji	kitchen
2520	naucila	learned
2521	ušuti	shut up
2522	objasnim	explain
2523	gomila	a bunch, crowd, heap, pile
2524	izdao	issued, published, given away
2525	vjerujemo	we believe
2526	voziš	driving
2527	ostalima	to others
2528	stigne	pinches
2529	shvacate	to understand
2530	traga	mark, trace
2531	dodemo	we come
2532	disati	breathe
2533	narocito	particularly, especially
2534	pse	dogs
2535	ponašaš	you behave
2536	cuva	keeps
2537	nivo	nobody
2538	vracaj	return
2539	hoces	you want, you will
2540	obuci	put on [clothing]
2541	parku	park
2542	sramota	shame, dishonor
2543	nadite	to find; to surpass
2544	povjerovati	to trust
2545	pocinjem	burst
2546	budale	fools
2547	ispricaj	excuse, explain
2548	uspije	fails
2549	napred	forward
2550	videli	see, have a look

2551	držimo	hold, retain, keep up, repute
2552	ponedjeljak	Monday
2553	osjecate	feel
2554	donosi	bringing
2555	pravog	real, right, straight
2556	upozorenje	warning, signal, premonition
2557	ubijaju	killing
2558	održati	to maintain, sustain, preserve
2559	snu	sleep, dream
2560	zapovijedi	command
2561	krenimo	let's start
2562	uzima	takes
2563	priznajem	I admit
2564	sposoban	capable, competent
2565	uzbudljivo	exciting
2566	casnik	officer
2567	slucajnost	coincidence
2568	projekt	plan, scheme
2569	upucao	shot
2570	znacilo	meant
2571	najvažnije	most important
2572	dnevno	daily, by the day
2573	ušla	entered
2574	postavio	posted by, set
2575	paket	package, packet, bundle
2576	otvorio	opened
2577	ponuditi	to offer, to propose
2578	razmišljala	she thought
2579	spremi	save
2580	bogat	rich, wealthy
2581	cinjenice	facts
2582	hrabar	brave
2583	istragu	investigation, inquest
2584	upaliti	light, ignite, turned on
2585	visok	excess, high, tall
2586	culo, culom	sense
2587	papire	papers
2588	pojaviti	appear
2589	gazda	boss, landlord, proprietor, owner
2590	dovedite	bring, take, lead
2591	dna	bottom, the bottom
2592	ucitelj	perpetrate
2593	slatki	sweet, sleek, cute
2594	udariti	to strike
2595	besplatno /tan	free, gratuitous,
2596	knjizi	book
2597	rijecima	in words
2598	zatvoren	closed
2599	izašla	gone out
2600	snova /e	dreams, again, sleep
2601	fotografije	photography

2602	sjecanja	memories
2603	veca	higher, bigger, more
2604	krila	wings
2605	umrli	died
2606	kurs	course
2607	predstava	show
2608	brz	quick, fast, rapid
2609	sjeti	remember
2610	vrate	door
2611	slušao	listen
2612	hlad	shade
2613	lmamo	we have
2614	sladoled	ice cream
2615	teorija	theory
2616	zidu	wall
2617	uništi	destroy, annihilate, wipe out
2618	razumije	understands
2619	nosila	stretcher
2620	funti	pounds
2621	zvijer	beast
2622	karijeru	career
2623	oprezno	carefully, warily
2624	prevod	translation
2625	onamo	there
2626	kvragu	hell
2627	teret	burden, load, cargo
2628	diši	dishes
2629	iznenada	suddenly, abruptly, by surprise
2630	plaži	beach
2631	starom	old
2632	vjencanja	weddings
2633	data	data
2634	razgovara	talks, converses
2635	vodom	water
2636	debeli	fat
2637	fali	miss
2638	udala	married
2639	onoj	the one, that
2640	crv	worm
2641	bolnica	hospital
2642	rec	word, speech
2643	istog	same
2644	pobjegla	escaped
2645	stavila /i	put, place, play
2646	zapovjednice	the generals, pawnshops,
2647	potpunosti	completely, entirely
2648	tijelu	the body
2649	zamolio	he asked, *zamoli* asks,
2650	govorili	talk, say, tell
2651	razgovarala	talking
2652	francuski	French

2653	sudenje	trial, judgement
2654	njihovih	their
2655	stignemo	we pinch
2656	ludilo	madness
2657	pomislila	she thought
2658	naocale	glasses
2659	muškaraca	men
2660	vecinu	most
2661	tvoga	your, yours
2662	crkv	churches
2663	rim	Rome
2664	srednje	medium
2665	javlja	occurs
2666	boj	battle
2667	zadovoljan	satisfied, *-ja* -ing, *zadovolj* satisfaction, *zadovol* satisfy
2668	vic	joke
2669	casni	honorable
2670	mrziš	you hate
2671	zaraditi	to earn
2672	puca	shoot, fire
2673	pomislil	he thought
2674	pitali	asked
2675	stižem	I'm coming
2676	provjerite	check
2677	dakako	of course, clearly
2678	klinci	kids
2679	osoblje	staff, personnel
2680	doveli	brought
2681	samu	alone
2682	zdravlje	health, hail
2683	cin	rank
2684	srecan	happy, lucky
2685	smiješan	funny
2686	tipom	type, make, mold
2687	povjerenje	confidence
2688	ocekuješ	you expect
2689	plati	pay
2690	kazna	discipline
2691	bezdan	abyss
2692	smetati	to bother, disturb, annoy
2693	andeo	angel, *andeo cuvar*, guardian angel
2694	lopov	thief
2695	junak	hero
2696	stupnjeva	degrees
2697	cinilo	it seemed
2698	prijeci	cross
2699	stil	style
2700	ukus	taste, flavor
2701	danima	days
2702	princeza	Princess
2703	svinja	pig, swine

2704	istoj	the same
2705	cijevi	tubing, tube,
2706	cinim	I am doing
2707	ukrasti	to steal
2708	bob /e	bean
2709	odu	I go
2710	zgodna	pretty
2711	pitate	you ask
2712	kcerka	daughter
2713	pozor	attention, get set, beware
2714	ponovi	say it again
2715	bakar	copper
2716	zaboravili	forgot
2717	vlastiti	own
2718	glasine	gossip, odor (!!)
2719	kužim	get it
2720	kožu	goat
2721	srecom	fortunately
2722	vlasti	authorities
2723	preveo	translate, translated, take across
2724	dopustio	allowed, permitted, tolerated, agreed
2725	prijedlog	proposal, proposition, suggestion
2726	nauditi	damage
2727	opas	belt
2728	živjela	lived
2729	prozora	window, window frame
2730	ledima	back
2731	vrh	top, apex, pinnacle
2732	lagala	lied
2733	dobitnik	winner
2734	izlazim	I'm going out, I'm leaving
2735	prešao	moved, crossed
2736	simbol	sign, token
2737	naredio	ordered, ordained, commanded
2738	plakati	to cry
2739	guzice	spanking
2740	uživati	you enjoy
2741	bum	boom, explosion,
2742	zamjenu	swap, *zamjen* exchange
2743	stopala	feet
2744	decku	deck
2745	ponašati	you behave
2746	bazi	basis
2747	stav	attitude, paragraph
2748	pobjeda	win, victory
2749	zacijelo	certainly,
2750	ukrali	stole
2751	posade	crew
2752	pocet	beginning
2753	parizu	Paris
2754	potpisati	sign, to sign

2755	lijekove	medicine
2756	pisao	wrote
2757	popij	drink
2758	društvu	society
2759	smisliti	devise, come up with
2760	subotu	Saturday, Sabbath, fur coat (?)
2761	pogotovo	especially
2762	prirodno	naturally
2763	stajao	standing, stood
2764	cetvrti	fourth
2765	primili	image, figure, character, archaetype
2766	mlijeko	milk
2767	okrenuti	rotate
2768	uciti	to study, learn
2769	secaš	remember, recall, dry
2770	paklu	hell
2771	gledamo	we watch, we see
2772	takvih	these
2773	milosti	grace, graciousness, favor, mercy
2774	cesta /e /i	road
2775	situaciji	circumstance
2776	istraživanje	research
2777	slab	weak
2778	bedro	thigh
2779	piješ	you drink
2780	njihovi	their
2781	cija	whose
2782	cas	hour
2783	lažem	lie
2784	poslednji	latest, lowest
2785	kaput	coat
2786	dobijemo	we get it
2787	ucitelju	perpetrators
2788	putovanja	travels
2789	saznali	found out
2790	pisac	writer
2791	majmuna	monkeys
2792	ponudio	offered
2793	praviti	make create, say
2794	igraju	play
2795	bodar	brisk
2796	zaštiti	to protect, protection, protect
2797	sluša	listen, hears
2798	teta	aunt
2799	zatvorite	close it
2800	utorak	Tuesday
2801	bojnice	Major
2802	svjestan	aware, deliberate, conscious
2803	rece	he said
2804	postici	achieve, mail
2805	robu	goods

2806	prostora	simply
2807	opasna	dangerous
2808	granica	border
2809	ubijte	assassinate
2810	nikakvih	no, none
2811	nedostajao	missing
2812	stola	stole
2813	plavi	blue
2814	pomoglo	helped
2815	pustili	release, allow, released
2816	listu	list
2817	uživajte	enjoy, delight, bask
2818	oženiti	to marry
2819	stvarnost	reality, actuality
2820	mesta	city
2821	želje	wishes, *želj* you will
2822	pogreška	error, mistake, lapse
2823	pomogla	helped
2824	djevojcice	girl, girls
2825	izabrati	choose
2826	prijetnja	pleasant
2827	otiske	prints, imprint, impression
2828	popio	drank, swallowed up
2829	vodiš	you lead
2830	pije	she drinks
2831	ženska	woman
2832	deca	children, the children
2833	ranjen	wounded, injured, stricken
2834	ynnol	copyright
2835	clanak	article
2836	želju	desire
2837	detalje	details
2838	objašnjava	explain
2839	pratim	follow, I follow, keep track of
2840	žrtava	victims
2841	decu	children
2842	goriva	fuel, propellant, combustibles
2843	posebna	special, distinct,
2844	zgodno	hurry
2845	klijent	client
2846	kanal	channel, canal
2847	strucnjak	loaf, experts
2848	stavim	insert, put upon
2849	obicna /e /i /u	ordinary
2850	starim	aging, getting odler
2851	viski	surplus, whiskey
2852	osjecala	felt
2853	vjerovala	faith, trust, believed
2854	umreš	die, expire
2855	terenu	field, grounds, terrain
2856	velikih	big, large

2857	kolega	colleague
2858	stavit	bet, wager
2859	greške	mistakes
2860	majmun	monkey
2861	odlazak	departure, check-out, exit
2862	crkva /e /i /o /u	church
2863	zatvorena	closed
2864	rezultate	results
2865	izjavu	statement, declaration, testimony
2866	brodom	boat
2867	obecaj	promise
2868	zasad	principles, for now, for the time being,
2869	rana /e	wound
2870	štiti	protects, shield
2871	cekala /e /i	waited
2872	dodji	come on
2873	takvog	such a

Notes on Serbo-Croat:

1. There is no such language. Serbo-Croat was a conglomoration of several related but distinct Slavic dialects. It was an official language of the late and unlamented Yugoslavia. Upon the dissolution of Yugoslavia, the Balkan Peninsula immediately Balkanized, creating a group of states, none of whom wish to acknowledge that they share a language with the others. As a result, Slovenian, Croatian, Bosnian, Montnegrin/Tsernagora, and Serbian are considered distinct languages, even though they have a 97% or higher interchangeability. This would be a bit like English speakers pretending that Canadian, Alabaman English, New Zealandish, and Australian were all distinct languages, unrelated to American or English. But the internationally-respected fiction is that all Slavic langauges are distinct, so let's pretend that's true.

2. In regards to note 1. above: For that matter, if you master Serbo-Croat, there is a distinct possiblity that you will notice a mild similarity to Slovakian, Slovenian, Czech, Bulgarian, Hungarian, Macedonian, Lithuanian and Polish. You might even (*Boge Moi!*) catch a few common words with Russian! But for goodness sake, don't ever say any of that out loud!

3. As a result of the fact that the distinct Slavic dialects of former Yugoslavia were once crammed together into the Bed of Procrustes known as Serbo-Croat, there are some linguistic oddities in Serbo-Croat. For example, there are at least seven billion and three words that independently translate as "God." In words that end in a vowel, a change of vowel may have exactly the same meaning, or it may not. Tata, Tate, Tati, and Tato all mean Dad or Daddy. But Tatu means thief. We hope that this is merely a coincidence. Where these words appear to all mean that same thing, or closely enough that it makes no difference, you may see **Tata /e /i /o** as the notation indicating interchangeability. With verbs, **-im** sometimes indicates first person singular, and **–imo** may mean first person plural. Or maybe not.

4. In other cases, a word may end with –a in one dialect (Croatian, perhaps) and –e in another (Serbian, perhaps). Or –e may indicate a plural noun. Or it may indicate that the typewriter being used lacked an –a key. Personally, I find it gratifying that there is at least one language in which the spelling rules make less sense than in English.

5. In researching the fact that a single word may have fifteen endings that all mean pretty much the same thing, I discovered that having a multitude of cases is common in Slavic languages. The accepted wisdom on learning the use cases – a concept largely foreign to Anglophones, as English has the bare minimum of cases necessary for clarity – is that one must spend extensive periods of complete immersion in the language. In other words, this is precisely the sort of language for which a book like this one is the best and most painless study guide. Learning the cases involved in Slavic language by means of classroom studies would be enough to make a person swear off all language learning forever, and possibly to swear off all use of language. I am quite certain that, somewhere in the mountains of Montenegro, there are tribes of former language students, driven mad by Serbo-Croat grammar, who now communicate solely by means of grunts and hand signals. There must be.

6. As a result of the above peculiarities, there are far more than 1000 words of Serbo-Croat listed in the preceding pages. Call it a bonus, based largely on the fact that I often could not decide which variants were distinct words, and which were merely affectations of a conglomerated-and-then-divided language. Oh, also, just to throw in another monkey wrench: Serbo-Croat can be written using the Western alphabet or the Cyrillic alphabet. Serbs and Bosnians lean towards the Cyrillic, Slovenes and Montnegrins towards the Western, and the Croatians can go either way. Herein, I have used only the Western alphabet.

7. As a result of all of the above, once again, this book is wrong. Just absolutely wrong. I've picked the wrong meaning for at least a few of these words, I'm certain. I think I used a few Lithuanian definitions when I really got desperate. Remember, the goal here is to get you started in the language, and not to make you its master, or even to prepare you for a trip. This is a primer: A starting point. I can't do all the work for you. Deal with it.

GERMAN / DEUTSCH:

Polite phrases and Important ideas:

Please	Bitte (BIHT-uh)
Thanks	Danke (Donk-a)
Thank you	Vielen Danke (VEEL-in DONK)
Thank you (emphasis)	Dankeschon (DONka-SHANE)
Welcome (after "Thanks")	Bitteschon (BIHT-uh SHANE)
Welcome (To a place)	Willkommen (WILL KOMM-inn)
Excuse me (interrupting)	Entschuldigen-sie (In-STHUl-duhgin-ZEE)
Pardon me (for an error)	Entschuldige mich (In-STHUl-duhgin MIHk)
Pardon me (for walking in front of someone)	Verzeih mir (VAIRTzigh Meer)
Forgive me (for a grave error)	Vergib mir (VAIRgib Meer)
I'm sorry	Es tut mir Leid (Es TOOT MEER Light)
What is your name?	Wie heissen sie? (Vee HIGH-SIN zee?)
My name is…	Ich heisse … (Ick-HIGH-suh) ("I call myself…")
Where are the restrooms?	Wo sind die Toiletten? (WOZEN-dee-toyLETTen?)

1	Ein (Ine)	6	Sechs (Zecks)	11	Elf (Elf)
2	Zvei (zVye)	7	Sieben (ZEEbin)	12	Dwolf (dWOOLf)
3	Drei (Dry)	8	Acht (Ocked)	13	Dreizehn (Dry-sin)
4	Vier (Fear)	9	Neun (Noon)	14	Vierzehn (Fear-sin)
5	Funf (FUNf)	10	Zehn (Zane)	15	Funfzehn (FUNf-sin)
16	Sechzehn (ZECT-sin)	21	Ein-und-zwanzig	70	Siebzig (ZEEBzig)
17	Siebzehn (ZEEB-sin)	30	Dreizig (DRYzig)	80	Achtzig (OCTzig)
18	Actzehn (Ocked-Sin)	40	Vierzig (FEARzig)	90	Neunzig (NOONzig)
19	Neun (NOON-sin)	50	Funfzig (FUNfzig)	100	Hundert (HOON-dairt)
20	Zwanzig (ZWAHNzigg)	60	Sechzig (ZECTzig)	1000	Tausend (TAHWsent)

10,000 Zehntausend (ZinnTAHWsent)   1,000,000 Million (MealYOON)   0 Null (Noill)

Odd Cases and Special Phrases:

Ich liebe dich – *I love you.*	(Ick LEEB Dichk)
Ich weiss es nicht – *I don't know*	(Ich WISE Ess nished) (lit: "I know it not)
Verstehen-sie?– *Do you understand?*. Verstehst du?	(VerSTAIN-zee?) (Intimate: VerSTEHisst DOO?)
Aber ja / Aber nein *But yes / but no*	(AhBurr YAH / AhBurr NINE)
Sei ruhig – *Be quiet!*	(Zye Ruy-sch)
Kommen-sie heir – *Come here*	(KOMMon-ZEE-here)

In GERMAN, sentences may be formed as Subject-Verb-Object (*Ich gehe dort hin*, I go there) but not Subject-Object-Verb. As in ENGLISH, noun modifiers are placed before the noun (*Grunes Auto*, green car, not *Auto grunes*, green car). Some verbs have an accusative ending –st (think of Shakespeare or the King James Bible): *glaubst du nicht?* (Thinkest thou not?) (Don't you think?). Verbs may become instructions with –sie (you) added as a suffix: *Kommen-sie* (Come-you), *Entschuldigen-sie, bitte* (Excuse-you, please).

Numbers above twenty use the form __-und-__zig, i.e. Vier-und-zwanzig (Four-and-twenty) ("Little Endian")

1	Der	The, which
2	Ich	I, me
3	Wie	As, like, such as
4	Das	the; that (one)
5	Du	You, also *sie*
6	Sie	You
7	Seine	His
8	Und	And
9	Dass	That
10	In	In, into
11	Ist	Is, to be
12	Den	The, That
13	Er	He
14	Nicht	No, not, nothing
15	Ja	Yes
16	Von	From, of
17	War	Was
18	Die	The (plural)
19	Fur	For
20	Auf	On, from, of, toward
21	Mit	With
22	Es	It
23	Im	In the
24	Sind	Are
25	So	So, thus
26	Was	What, which
27	Des	Of
28	Sein	Be
29	Wir	We
30	Bei	At, in
31	Ein	A, one
32	Noch	Still, yet, more
33	Sich	Such, as such, in itself, yourself
34	Zu	To, for, at, with
35	Da	There, here; since, because
36	Dem	The
37	Hab, habe, haben	Have, Possess, Possessions
38	Mir	Me, to me, myself
39	Dies	This
40	Mal	Times; once
41	Aus	From, out, out of, off
42	Auch	Also, too
43	Durch	By
44	Heiss	Hot
45	Wort	Word
46	Aber	But, however
47	Nein	No
48	Mich	Me, to me, myself
49	Doch	But
50	Eine, einem, einer	A, One
51	Einige	Some

52	Hier	Here
53	Schon	Already
54	Dir	You, to you, yourself
55	Fur	For
56	Man	One, they
57	Oder	Or
58	Hatte	Had
59	Dann	Then, in that case
60	Hast	Haste
61	Hat	Have
62	Dich	You, yourself
63	Wenn	When, If, That one time
64	An	To, for, at, with
65	Konnen	Can, may, might
66	Andere, anderen	Other
67	Bin	Be
68	Waren	Were
69	Nur	Only, solely, simply
70	Tun	Do
71	Ihre	Their, your
72	Ihr	Here
73	Zeit	Time, age, *Zeitgeist*, spirit of the age, popular trend
74	Gut, gute, guten	Good, well
75	Werden	will, *werder* Become
76	Uns	Us
77	Sagte	Said, told
78	Jetzt	Now
79	Ihn	Him, he
80	Jeder	Each, any, every
81	Sagen	Tell, say
82	Kann, kannst	Can, *kannst du?* can you? *Kannst du nicht?* Can you not?
83	Tut	Does
84	Satz	Set
85	Drei	Three
86	Wollen	Want
87	Denn	Because, then
88	Luft	Air
89	Spielen	Play
90	Klein, kleine	Small, little
91	Mein, meine	My
92	Ende	End
93	Als	Than
94	Setzen	Put
95	Weiss	White
96	Um	Around
97	Zuhause	Home
98	Lesen	Read
99	Wirklich	Really
100	Seits	Hand
101	Bist	To be, *du bist* you are
102	Hafen	Port

103	Gross, grosse	Large, size
104	Wird	Shall
105	Also	So, thus, also
106	Buchstabieren	Spell
107	Kein, keine, keinen	Not, no, *keine ahnung* no idea, *keine sorge* don't worry
108	Hinzufugen	Add
109	Nach	After
110	Alles	Everything, all
111	Lande	Land
112	muss	Must
113	Nichts	Nothing
114	Sehr	Very
115	Hoch	High, tall
116	Wieder	Again
117	Wo	Where
118	Folgen	Follow
119	Akt	Act
120	Bitte	Please
121	Geht	Goes, *geht nicht* goes not, *geht es dir gut?* Are you alright?
122	Warum	Why
123	Frag, fragen	Ask
124	Mehr	More
125	Manner	Men
126	Ihnen	Them
127	Veranderung	Change
128	Ging	Went
129	Etwas	Something
130	Euch	To you, *euch auch* to you as well
131	Licht	Light
132	Art	Type, kind
133	Einfach	Easy
134	Ganz	Quite
135	Los	Come on
136	Massen	Need
137	Haus, hause	House
138	Immer	Always
139	Bild	Picture
140	Vor	Before, ago, afore
141	Ach	Oh
142	Mann	Man
143	Versuchen	Try
144	Zum	To the
145	Weide	Pasture
146	Tier	Animal
147	Punkt	Point
148	Sehen	See
149	Danke	Thanks, *danke* thank you, *dankeschon* thank you
150	Mutter	Mother
151	Welt	World
152	Gehen	Go, walk,
153	Nahe	Near

154	Werd, werde	Will, *werde ich* I will,
155	Bauen	Build
156	Wer	Who, *wer bist du?* who are you?
157	Selbst	Self
158	Soll	Should
159	Erde	Earth
160	Vater	Father
161	Wieso	How so?
162	Ihm	Him, he
163	Warde	Would
164	Konnen	Can, be capable
165	Neu, neue, neuen, neues	New
166	Weil	Because
167	Arbeit	Work
168	Diese	These
169	Gott	God, *Gott sei denk* thank God, *Gottesdienst* church service
170	Komm	Come over, come on
171	Teil	Part
172	Gar	At all, really
173	Nehmen	To take
174	Erhalten	Get
175	Vielleicht	Perhaps
176	Ort	Place
177	Gemacht	Made
178	Willst	Want, *willst du* what do you want?
179	Leben	Live, life
180	Gibt	Gives
181	Leid	Suffering
182	Nie	Never
183	Uber	Over
184	Viel, viele	Much, many, lots
185	Zuruck	Back
186	Wenig	Little
187	Runde	Round
188	Jahr, jahre	Year
189	Weg	Path
190	Deine, deinem, deinen	Yours
191	Kam	Came
192	Wollte	Wanted to
193	Nun	Now, *nun ja* oh well
194	Zeigen	Show
195	Wissen	Know
196	Am	At the
197	Geben	Give, Given
198	Gesagt	Said
199	Unser, unsere	Our
200	Heute	Today, *heute abend* this evening
201	Unter	Under
202	Frau	Lady, woman, wife, Mrs.
203	Komme, kommen	Come
204	Kommt	is coming, *kommt drauf an* depends on, *kommt schon* come on

205	Gern	Gladly
206	Mussen	Have to, required
207	Formular	Form
208	Denken	Think
209	Hallo	Hello
210	Hilfe	Help
211	Niedrig	Low
212	Ware	Goods, esp. goods for sale
213	Wurde	Honor
214	Linie	Line
215	Abweichen	Differ
216	Dein	Your, thine
217	Wiederum	Turn
218	Ursache	Cause
219	Alle, Alles	All
220	Bis	Until
221	Bedeuten	Mean, signify
222	Klar	Clear
223	Macht	Power, *macht nicht* doesn't matter
224	Umzug	Move
225	Recht	Right
226	finde, findest	Discover, encounter
227	Junge	Boy
228	Alt	Old
229	Damit	In order to, so that
230	Gleich	Same, equal
231	Dieser, Dieses, Diesem	This
232	Genau	Exact
233	Oben	Up
234	He	Hey, you there!
235	Verwendung	Use
236	Wohl	Health, wellbeing
237	Zwei	Two
238	Meinen	Do you mean?
239	Gerade	Straight
240	Sicher	Safe, secure, certain
241	Naturlich	Naturally
242	Schreiben	Write, written, letter, document
243	Weisst	Knows
244	Morgen	Morning
245	Ab	From
246	Liebe	Love, dear
247	Lassen	Let, allow
248	Hor	Listen, *hor mal zu* Listen
249	Lang, lange	Long
250	Leute	People
251	Zur	To *zurzeit* for now.
252	Geld	Money
253	Sache	Thing
254	Essen	Eat
255	Zusammen	Together

256	Mochte	Would like to
257	Suchen	Look
258	Toll, tolle, toller	Great, amazing
259	Tag	Day
260	Konnte, konnten,	Could, *konnte nicht* could not
261	Musst, musste	Must, *musst klappen* should work
262	Raus	Out
263	Wirst	Will
264	Konnte	Can, be capable
265	Tat	Did
266	Anzahl	Number
267	Beide, beiden	Both
268	Klingen	Sound
269	Wohltat	Kindness, charity
270	Gesehen	Seen, *gesehen haben*, has seen
271	Ob	Whether
272	Meisten	Most *am meisten* at the most
273	Menschen	People, mankind
274	Sollte	Should
275	Glaube	Faith
276	Nett	Kind
277	Her	Forth
278	Wasser	Water
279	Dachte	Could
280	Sag	Say
281	Anruf	Call
282	Reden	Speaking
283	Erst, erste	First
284	Meiner	Mine, *meiner mienung* my opinion
285	Besser	Better
286	Ohne	Without
287	Unten	Down
288	Jemand -en -em	Someone, somebody, anyone, anybody
289	Seite	Side
290	Gewesen	Been
291	Paar	Pair
292	Passiert	Happens
293	Finden	Find
294	Habt	Have, *habt ihr* do you have
295	Freund, freunde	Friend
296	Kopf	Head
297	Gehert, gehort	Heard
298	Stehen	Stand
299	Besitzen	Own
300	Dort	There
301	Sagt	Says
302	Warte	Wait
303	Land	Country
304	Eigentlich	Actually
305	Gefunden	Found
306	Antwort	Answer

307	Hor	Listen
308	Bestimmt	Certainly
309	Schule	School
310	Wachsen	Grow
311	Diesen	This one
312	Sollten	Should
313	Studie	Study
314	Ins	In the
315	Lernen	Learn
316	Anlage	Plant
317	Richtig	Correct
318	Abdeckung	Cover
319	Weiter	Further, *weiterhin* farther on
320	Eben	Just
321	Lebensmittel	Food
322	Vom	From, of
323	Sonne	Sun
324	Darf	May
325	Herr	Mister
326	Vier	Four
327	Meinem	My, mine
328	Zwischen	Between
329	Warst	Were, *warst du?* were you?
330	Zustand	State, condition
331	Halten	Keep, hold, stay
332	Ordnung	Order, orderliness, rechtitude
333	Auge	Eye
334	Frage	Question
335	Letzte	Latest
336	Bisschen	Little, a little bit
337	Gedanken	Thought
338	Madchen	Maiden, girl, young woman
339	Lieber	Dear, *lieber kunde* dear customer
340	Stadt	City, town
341	Baum	Tree
342	Horen	Listen
343	Uberqueren	Cross
344	Sieht	Sees
345	Bauernhof	Farm
346	Schwer	Hard, heavy
347	Beginn	Start
348	Hin	There
349	Seit	Since
350	Geschichte	Story, history
351	Abend	Evening
352	Sage	Saw
353	Weit	Far
354	Meer	Sea
355	Lass, lasse	Let, allow, *lassen sie mich wissen* let me know
356	Ziehen	Draw, pull
357	Links	Left

358	Hort	Hoard, trove
359	Spat	Late
360	Laufen	Run
361	Unterlassen	Refrain, omit, fail
362	Angst	Fear, anxiety
363	Mach, mache, machen	Make, do
364	Wahrend	While, during, whereas
365	Kenne, kennen	Know, *kennerlernen* to get to know, *kenner wir uns?* Do we know each other?
366	Presse	Press
367	Schliessen	Close
368	Vergessen	To forget, *vergessenheit* oblivion
369	Dubei	Over there
370	Nacht	Night
371	Realen	Real
372	Tja	Well
373	Wenige	Few
374	Norden	North
375	Bleiben	Stay
376	Buch	Book
377	Tot	Dead
378	Tragen	Carry
379	Unglaublich	Unbelieveable
380	Nahm	Took
381	Siehst	See
382	Super	Great, *supermarkt* supermarket
383	Wissenschaft	Science
384	Rein	Purely, *reinigen* clean, *reinigung* cleaning
385	Wahr	True
386	Zimmer	Room
387	Begann	Began
388	Davon	From that
389	Machst	Do you? *Machst du sport?* Do you play sports? *Machst du witze?* Are you kidding?
390	Idee	Idea
391	Fisch	Fish
392	Sollen	Should, *sollen wir* should we
393	Berg	Mountain
394	Frauen	Women
395	Helfen	Help, *helfen sie mir* help me
396	Schnell	Quick
397	Stopp	Stop
398	Einmal	Once
399	Kind	Child, baby, offspring
400	Basis	Base
401	Eines, eins	One
402	Daruber	About that...
403	Horen	Hear
404	Pferd	Horse
405	Sieh	See
406	Meinst	Mean, *meinst du?* Do you mean?
407	Schnitt	Cut
408	Wegen	Because of

409	Wohnung	Flat, apartment, living space
410	Beobachten	Watch
411	Verstehe	Understand?
412	Allein	Alone, by itself
413	Farbe	Color
414	Stimmt	Correct, *stimmt nicht* it's not true, *Stimmt das?* Is that true?
415	Dafur	For this
416	Gesicht	Face
417	Wardest	To be
418	Holz	Wood
419	Steht	Stands, *steht auf* stands up
420	Haupt-	Main
421	Kerl	Guy, fellow, dude
422	Kinder	Children
423	Geoffnet	Open
424	Genug	Enough
425	Seid	Are
426	Scheinen	Seem
427	Sonst	Else
428	Ganze, ganzen	Whole
429	Halt	Stop
430	Nachste, nachsten	Next
431	Sei	Be
432	Zwar	Though, *Zwar aber* indeed ... But
433	Gegen	Against
434	Start	Begin
435	Bekam	Got
436	Beispiel	Example
437	Denke	Think, believe, feel
438	Etwa	About
439	Blick	Sight, view
440	Erleichtern	Ease
441	Papier	Paper
442	Wisst	Know, *wisst ihr?* do you know?
443	Gruppe	Group
444	Ihren	Their
445	Glaub, glauben	Believe
446	Bringen	Bring
447	Musik	Music
448	Diejenigen	Those
449	Bekommen	To obtain
450	Niemand	No one
451	Marke	Mark
452	Warten	Wait
453	Brauchen	Need, require, have need of
454	Heiraten	Marry
455	Daran	About it
456	Meile	Mile
457	Fluss	River
458	Wann	When
459	Auto	Car

460	Heisst	Called
461	Faue	Lazy
462	Klasse	Class
463	Sprechen	Speak
464	Pflege	Care
465	Zweite	Second
466	Verruckt	Insane
467	Ebene	Plain
468	Sofort	Immediately
469	Getan	Done
470	Solltest	Should?
471	Ublich	Usual
472	Fertig	Finished, ready, through
473	Jung	Young
474	Bereit	Ready
475	Oben	Open, Above
476	Sohn	Son
477	Freundin	Girlfriend, lover
478	Je	Ever
479	Rot	Red
480	Liste	List
481	Jahren	Years
482	Obwohl	Though
483	Beim	At the
484	Fuhlen, fuhlst	Feel, sense
485	Seinen, seinem, seiner	His
486	Vortrag	Talk
487	Wusste	Knew
488	Mag	Like
489	Vallig	Completely
490	Vogel	Bird
491	Bald	Soon
492	Gefahl, gefahle	Feelings
493	Korper	Body
494	Hatten	Would have
495	Hund	Dog
496	Familie	Family
497	Vielen	Many
498	Bevor	Before
499	Direkt	Direct
500	Spass	Fun
501	Bruder	Brother
502	Pose	Pose
503	Verlassen	Leave
504	Lied	Song
505	Messen	Measure
506	Tar	Door
507	Produkt	Product
508	Uhr	Hour, clock
509	Schwarz	Black
510	Kurz	Short

511	Schwester	Sister
512	Kriegen	Obtain
513	Zahl	Numeral
514	Wind	Wind
515	Gedacht	Thought
516	Passieren	Happen, pass
517	Spater	Later
518	Geller	Right
519	Vollstandig	Complete
520	Runter	Down, *runtergefallen* fell down
521	Schiff	Ship
522	Bereich	Area
523	Fahren	Drive, lead, guide
524	Halfte	Half
525	Warden	To be
526	Furchtbar	Awful, frightful, shocking
527	Stein	Rock, stone
528	Bestellen	Order
529	Feuer	Fire
530	Namen	Names, naming
531	Dank	Thanks, *danke* thank you, *dankeschon* thank you
532	Saden	South
533	Sehe	See
534	Augen	Onto
535	Gab	Gave
536	Stack	Piece
537	Dazu	To that, for that
538	Wurden	Honors
539	Irgendwie	Somehow
540	Obere	Top
541	Entschuldige	Excuse
542	Egal	No matter
543	Konig	King
544	Strasse	Street
545	Zoll	Inch
546	Multiplizieren	Multiply
547	Sterben	Die
548	Konnten	Could, can
549	Kurs	Course
550	Jungs	Guys, young men
551	Bett	Bed
552	Jeden	Everyone, *jeden tag* every day
553	Rad	Wheel
554	Uberhaupt	Over all, anyhow, anyway
555	Minuten	Minutes
556	Voll	Full
557	Kraft	Force
558	Verstehen	Understand
559	Blau	Blue
560	Treffen	Meet
561	Objekt	Object

562	Entscheiden	Decide
563	Oberflache	Surface
564	Spiel	Game, match, sport
565	Tief	Deep
566	Mond	Moon
567	Nimm	Take
568	Insel	Island
569	Fuss	Foot
570	Gluck	Luck
571	Gefallen	Like, *gefallen mir* I like, *gefallen tun* oblige
572	System	System
573	Beschaftigt	Busy, employed, occupied
574	Eltern	Parents
575	Prafung	Test
576	Rekord	Record
577	Ruhig	Quiet
578	Typ	Type
579	Boot	Boat
580	Daruber	About that, concerning which
581	Gemeinsam	Common
582	Goldenen	Golden
583	Sachen	Stuff
584	Moglich	Possible
585	Tur	Door
586	Flugzeug	Plane
587	Deswegen	Because of that
588	Statt	Stead
589	Bloss	Just
590	Trocken	Dry
591	Sah	Saw
592	Wunder	Wonder
593	Ernst	Serious
594	Lachen	Laugh
595	Seht	Look
596	Tausend	Thousand
597	Eure	Your, yours
598	Kaffee	Coffee
599	Lief	Ran
600	Ruhe	Quiet, *ruhestand* retirement, *ruhig* calm
601	Uberprufen	Check
602	Gestern	Yesterday, *gestern abend* last night
603	Ihrer	Of their
604	Form	Shape
605	Gleichsetzen	Equate
606	Witzig	Funny
607	Toten	Dead, *totenkopf* skull, *totenschein* death certificate
608	Fall	Case
609	Fehl	Miss
610	Gebracht	Brought
611	Verheiratet	Married
612	Polizei	Police

613	Warme	Heat
614	Liegt	Lies
615	Schnee	Snow
616	Vorbei	Gone
617	Gluck	Luck, fortune, happiness
618	Krieg	War
619	Reifen	Tire
620	Darauf	Thereupon
621	Entfernt	Distant
622	Fullen	Fill
623	Vetter	Male cousin
624	Osten	East
625	Endlich	At last, finally
626	Malen	Paint
627	Dran	Turn on
628	Sprache	Language
629	Einheit	Unit
630	Momentan	Currently, right away
631	Leider	Unfortunately
632	Sagst	Say *sagst du?* Do you say?
633	Fein	Fine
634	Schau	Look, watch
635	Gefillt	Filled
636	Sogar	Even
637	Fliegen	Fly
638	Fallen	Fall, drop
639	Fahren	Drive, lead, guide
640	Hinter	Behind
641	Drin	In there
642	Schrei	Cry
643	Teufel	devil, demon
644	Dunkel	Dark
645	Keiner	None, *keiner weiss* nobody knows, *keiner da* no one is there
646	Maschine	Machine
647	Wollt	Want
648	Mittegessen	Lunch
649	Falsch	Wrong
650	Vergnugen	Pleasure
651	Abbildung	Figure
652	Hort	Heard
653	Stern	Star
654	Kasten	Box
655	Nomen	Noun
656	Feld	Field
657	Kommst	Come, *kommst du* are you coming? *Kommst du mit?* Coming with me?
658	Einladen	Invite, *einladung* invitation
659	Gib	Give
660	Woher	Where from, *woher kommst du?* where do you come from?
661	Fahig	Able
662	Ihrem	Their
663	Pfund	Pound

664	Telefon	Telephone
665	Wagen	Dare
666	Arbeiten	Work, operate
667	Erzahlt	Tells
668	Schonheit	Beauty
669	Antriebs	Drive
670	Stand	Stood
671	Tod	Death
672	Enthalten	Contain
673	Hattest	Would have
674	Echt	Really, real
675	Bleistift	Pencil
676	Lehren	Teach
677	Wichtig	Important
678	Irgendwas	Anything, whatever
679	Woche	Week
680	Bringt	Brings
681	Finale	Final
682	Braucht	Needs
683	Grun	Green
684	Nomlich	Normal
685	Gerne	With pleasure
686	Bedeutet	Means, signifies
687	Draussen	Outside, see also *ausserhalb*
688	Entwickeln	Develop
689	Funf	Five
690	Ozean	Ocean
691	Abgemacht	Agreed
692	Fassen	Grasp, touch, take, fasten
693	Kostenlos	Free
694	Gasthaus	Inn, also *gasthof*
695	Stark	Strong
696	Besondere	Special
697	Geist	Mind
698	Verstanden	Understood, *verstanden habe.* Have understood
699	Wohnen	Live, live in
700	Anders	Different
701	Schwanz	Tail
702	Sorgen	To care
703	Produzieren	Produce
704	Welche	Which
705	Augenblick	Moment, instant, current instant
706	Einzige	Only one
707	Tatsache	Fact
708	Raum	Space
709	Vorstellen	Imagine
710	Beste	Best
711	Verloren	Lost
712	Ahnung	Idea, notion
713	Stunde	Hour
714	Alter	Aged

715	Ziemlich	Pretty
716	Gekommen	Came, arrived, were brought
717	Wiedersehen	See you again, also *wiedersehn*
718	Hundert	Hundred
719	Lauft	Running
720	Funf	Five
721	Gehst	Going, *gehst du?* Are you going?
722	Grossartig	Great
723	Merken	Remember
724	Schritt	Step
725	Fruh	Early *fruher* earlier
726	Trinken	To drink
727	Westen	West
728	Boden	Ground, bottom, floor, soil
729	Interesse	Interest
730	Darum	Therefore, that is why
731	Erreichen	Reach
732	Tage	Days
733	Verbum	Verb
734	Sasse	Sit
735	Singen	Sing
736	Hand	Held
737	Sechs	Six
738	Tabelle	Table, chart
739	Bliebt	Remains, stays, keeps
740	Reise	Travel
741	Tochter	Daughter
742	Weniger	Less
743	Lust, lustig	Funny
744	Guter	Goods
745	Zehn	Ten
746	Grund	Reason, grounds
747	Mehrere	Several
748	Anrufen	To Call
749	Vokal	Vowel
750	Nummer	Number
751	Schlecht	Bad, *schlecter*, worse
752	Schatz	Treasure, *Schatzi* Sweetheart
753	Deshalb	That's why
754	Legen	Lay
755	Find	Locate
756	Holen	To collect, to retrieve
757	Hoffe	Hope
758	Muster	Pattern
759	Schleppend	Slow
760	Glucklich	Happy, lucky
761	Zentrum	Center
762	Wolltest	Wanted
763	Gefallt	Like, *gefallen mir* I like, *gefallen tun* oblige
764	Dienen	Serve
765	Wahnsinnig	Insane

766	Erscheinen	Appear
767	Lasst	Leaves, *lasst mich* allow me
768	Karte	Map
769	schluss	Enough, *schlussfolgerung* conclusion
770	Stunden	Hours, *stundenplan* timetable
771	Herz	Heart
772	Regen	Rain
773	Regel	Rule
774	Tisch	Table, *tische* tables
775	Wohin	Where, *Wohin willst du?* Where do you want to go?
776	Geworden	Become, *geworden ist* has become
777	Regieren	Govern
778	Kalte	Cold
779	Unbedingt	Absolutely
780	Hinweis	Notice
781	Sturmglocke	Alarm bell
782	Komisch	Funny, strange, weird
783	Stimme	Voice
784	Energie	Energy
785	Jagd	Hunt, *Jaeger* Hunter
786	streifen	Glance, touch in passing
787	wahrscheinlich	Probable
788	Ei	Egg
789	Spitz	Pointed, sharp
790	Drauf	On it
791	Fahrt	Ride
792	Ding	Thing, *ding-in-such* the thing itself
793	Zelle	Cell
794	Anderes	Other
795	Liebschaft	Love affair
796	Pflacken	Pick
797	Schlafen	Sleep, sleeping
798	Lossprechen	Absolve, acquit
799	Platzlich	Sudden
800	Zahlen	Pay or count, see *Zahlung*
801	Platz	Square
802	Dauer	Length
803	Vertreten	Represent
804	Brauchst	Need
805	Kunst	Art
806	Thema	Subject
807	Evangelische	Protestant
808	Beziehung	Relationship, also *anziehung*
809	Grosse	Size, weight, large
810	Variieren	Vary
811	Regeln	Settle
812	Gewicht	Weight
813	Kennst	You know, *kennst du mich* Do you know me? *kennst du das?* Did you know?
814	Allgemein	In general, generally
815	Eis	Ice
816	Materie	Matter

817	Kreis	Circle
818	Mensch	Human
819	Umfassen	Include
820	Erzahlen, erzahl	Tell
821	Kluft	Divide
822	Arzt	Doctor
823	Silbe	Syllable
824	Filz	Felt
825	Leicht	Light, *lutz leicht* bright light
826	Kugel	Ball
827	Richtige	Right, correct
828	Welle	Wave
829	Darfst	May
830	Vorhanden	Present
831	Vorhin	Earlier
832	Ringen	Wrestle
833	Tanz	Dance
834	Motor	Engine
835	Rede	Speech
836	Kusine	Female cousin
837	Lieb	Dear
838	Breit	Wide
839	Kussen	To kiss, to touch tangentially
840	Segel	Sail
841	Material	Material
842	Witz	Joke
843	Fraktion	Fraction
844	Wald	Forest
845	Sitzen	Sit
846	Rennen	Race
847	Fenster	Window
848	Rolle	Roll
849	Speicher	Store
850	Hochzeit	Wedding
851	Sommer	Summer
852	Entschuldigen	Excuse
853	Zug	Train
854	Schlaf	Sleep
855	Beweisen	Prove
856	Einsam	Lone
857	Bein	Leg
858	Ãœbung	Exercise
859	Lieben	Love, *lieben denke* heartfelt thanks
860	Wand	Wall
861	Fang	Catch
862	Gewonnen	Won
863	Wunschen	Wish
864	Himmel	Sky, heavens, heaven
865	Ehrlich	Honest
866	Freude	Joy
867	Wollten	Wanted to

131

868	Blutig	Rare, underdone
869	Sa	Sat
870	Geschrieben	Written
871	Niemals	No way!
872	Wilden	Wild
873	Instrument	Instrument
874	Manchmal	Sometimes
875	Geburtstag	Birthday
876	Gehalten	Kept
877	Glas	Glass
878	Miteinander	Together
879	Gras	Grass
880	Kuh	Cow
881	Fest	Firmly, festival
882	Damals	Back then
883	Rand	Edge
884	Zeichen	Sign, symbol
885	Besuch	Visit
886	Unterhalten	Beneath, underneath,
887	Vergangenheit	Past
888	Weich	Soft
889	Konntest	Could, *konntest du schlafen?* Could you sleep?
890	Hell	Bright, vivid, lucid
891	Gases	Gas
892	Wetter	Weather
893	Anfangen	To begin
894	Monat	Month
895	Neffen	Nephew
896	Werdet	Will
897	Verstehst	Understand? *Verstehst du mich?* Do you understand me?
898	Hoffen	Hope *hoffen wir* hope for
899	Blume	Flower
900	Gesprochen	Spoken
901	Kleiden	Clothes
902	Tanzen	To dance
903	Jedenfalls	In any case, *jedenfalls nicht* at least not
904	Seltsam	Strange
905	Geschlafen	Slept
906	Durfen	Allowed to
907	Handel	Trade
908	Melodie	Melody
909	Kaufen	Buy
910	Buro	Office
911	Hol	Fetch, retrieve
912	Empfangen	Receive
913	Findet	Finds
914	Reihe	Row
915	Mund	Mouth
916	Schwanger	Pregnant *schwangerschaft* pregnancy
917	Kriege	Get, acquire
918	Wenigsten	Least *am wenigsten* at the least

919	Arger	Trouble
920	Glaubst	Trust, suppose, *glaubst du nicht* don't you think?
921	Ausser	Except
922	Fantastisch	Fantastic, terrific, incredible
923	Denkt	Thinks
924	Schrieb	Wrote
925	Samen	Seed
926	Allen	Everyone
927	Ton	Tone
928	Beitreten	Join
929	Zuerst	First
930	Tust	Do, act, put
931	Vorschlagen	Suggest
932	Sauber	Clean
933	Pause	Break
934	Dame	Lady
935	Gefragt	Asked, *gefragt sein* to be in demand
936	Hof	Yard
937	Fand	Found
938	Steigen	Rise
939	Schlag	Blow
940	Ol	Oil
941	Seh	See
942	Blut	Blood
943	Ruf	Call
944	Berahren	Touch
945	Rach	Vengeance, *rache* revenge, (see Doyle, *A Study in Scarlet*)
946	Letzten	Last, most recent
947	Wuchs	Grew
948	Cent	Cent
949	Bose	Angry
950	Mischen	Mix
951	Besten	Best *am besten* for the best
952	Mannschaft	Team
953	Draht	Wire
954	Kosten	Cost
955	Vergiss	Forget
956	Braun	Brown
957	Heissen	Hot, it is called
958	Garten	Garden
959	Gesendet	Sent
960	Hintern	Rear, bottom, behind
961	Wahlen	Choose, select, elect
962	Fiel	Fell
963	Gelernt	Learned
964	Passen	Fit
965	Fliessen	Flow
966	Messe	Fair
967	Ansehen	Look at, notice, observe
968	Sammeln	Collect
969	Sparen	Save

970	Kontrolle	Control
971	Reicht	Enough, *reichtum* wealth
972	Dezimal	Decimal
973	Nehme	Take
974	Haltst	Hold, keep
975	Ohr	Ear
976	Gegangen	Went, *gefangen ist* has gone
977	Pleite	Broke, *bankrott* bankrupt
978	Ward	Was
979	Mittel	Middle
980	Wartet	Wait
981	Totten	Kill
982	Unserer	Ours
983	Peinlich	Embarrassing
984	See	Lake
985	Getroffen	Met, *getroffen werden* to be struck
986	Maustab	Scale
987	Autoren	Authors
988	Laut	Loud
989	Fruhling	Spring
990	Unsinn	Nonsense
991	Konsonant	Consonant
992	Mochtest	Liked
993	Kaum	Barely, *kaum zu glauben* hard to believe
994	Abendgessen	Dinner
995	Warterbuche	Dictionary
996	Milch	Milk
997	Verliebt	In Love
998	Geschwindigkeit	Speed
999	Schwierig	Difficult
1000	Verfahren	Lost
1001	Orgel	Organ
1002	Schrecklich	Dreadful
1003	Schlimm	Bad
1004	Zahlung	Payment, *zahlunsart* payment method
1005	Abschnitt	Section
1006	Kleid	Dress
1007	Kriegst	Go get
1008	Hubsch	Pretty
1009	Wolke	Cloud
1010	Uberraschung	Surprise
1011	Grosser	Larger
1012	Fahl, fahle	Pale
1013	Winzig	Tiny
1014	Aufstieg	Climb
1015	Denen	To them, to those
1016	Kuhlen	Cool, *kuhler* cooler
1017	Entwurf	Design
1018	Verabredet	Arranged, agreed
1019	Arm, arme	Poor
1020	Tu	Do

1021	Menge	Lot, crowd, gaggle
1022	Versuch	Experiment
1023	Schauspieler	Actor (literally "Look-player")
1024	Eisen	Iron
1025	Nachher	Later
1026	Einzel	Single
1027	Funktioniert	Working, operational, fuctional
1028	Froh	Glad
1029	Kreige	Create
1030	Zwanzig	Twenty
1031	Haut	Skin
1032	Lacheln	Smile
1033	Falte	Crease
1034	Loch	Hole
1035	Wem	Whom *wem gehort das* To whom does this belong?
1036	Springen	Jump
1037	Trotzdem	Nevertheless
1038	Acht	Eight
1039	Dorf	Village
1040	Standig	Constantly
1041	Spielt	Plays
1042	Kleines	Little one, *kleines madchen* little girl
1043	Wurzel	Root
1044	Kapiert	Got it, understood
1045	Erhahen	Raise
1046	Interessiert	Interested
1047	Grossen	Huge
1048	Losen	Solve, *auflosen* dissolve, resolve, *aufklaren* explain, clarify
1049	Gekasst	Cashed
1050	Metall	Metal
1051	Ynnol	Copyright
1052	Dracken	Push
1053	Antrag	Application
1054	Sieben	Seven
1055	Absatz	Paragraph
1056	Angerufen	Called
1057	Dritte	Third
1058	Vorher	Before, *vorhersage* forecast
1059	Versteh	Understand
1060	Haar, haare	Hair
1061	Beschreiben	Describe
1062	Sorge	Worry
1063	Koch	Cook
1064	Sollst	Should *sollstunden* target hours
1065	Entweder	Either
1066	Nennen	Mention
1067	Ergebnis	Result
1068	Klingt	Sounds
1069	Brennen	Burn
1070	Kleiner	Smaller, *kleiner bruder* little brother
1071	Geschafft	Made, *geschafft haben* did it, *geschaffen* created

1072	Hugel	Hill
1073	Erfahren	Experienced
1074	Entschuldigung	Sorry
1075	Katze	Cat
1076	Affen	Monkeys
1077	Jahrhundert	Century
1078	Absolut	Absolutely
1079	Betrachten	Consider
1080	Gesetz	Law
1081	Spitzer	Sharpener
1082	Kuste	Coast
1083	Kopie	Copy
1084	Ausdruck	Phrase
1085	Still	Silent
1086	Wenigstens	At least
1087	Konte	Count, account for
1088	Wahnsinn	Madness
1089	Stellen	To place, arrange, put,
1090	Schuld	Fault, *schuldig* guilty, *schuldigen* owe
1091	Redest	To talk
1092	Temperatur	Temperature
1093	Nackt	Naked
1094	Industrie	Industry
1095	Merkwurdig	Strange
1096	Meinte	Meant
1097	Wert	Value
1098	Jungen	Boys, children
1099	Kampf	Fight, struggle, burden
1100	Irgendwann	Sometime, someday
1101	Luge	Lie
1102	Geschenk, geschenke	Gift, gifts
1103	Schlagen	Beat
1104	Begeistern	Excite
1105	Fehler	Error, fault, mistake
1106	Aufs	Onto
1107	Sinn	Sense
1108	Hauptstadt	Capital
1109	Sekunde	Second
1110	Wird nicht	Won't
1111	Stuhl	Chair
1112	Achtung	Attention, warning, danger
1113	Obst	Fruit
1114	Kriegt	Gets
1115	Reich	Rich
1116	Dick	Thick
1117	Genauso	Just like that
1118	Soldat	Soldier
1119	Gegeben	Given, factual, *gegebenfalls* possibly, *gegebenhat* has given
1120	Prozess	Process
1121	Betreiben	Operate
1122	Ehe	Marriage

1123	All	Universe, space
1124	Praxis	Practice
1125	Trennen	Separate
1126	Schatzen	Protect
1127	Gemeint	Meant
1128	Mittag	Noon
1129	Ernte	Crop
1130	Fallt	Falls, *falltur* trap door
1131	Modernen	Modern
1132	Elementes	Element
1133	Denk	Think, think of, conceive
1134	Schaler	Student
1135	Ecke	Corner
1136	Partei	Party
1137	Versorgung	Supply
1138	Wochen	Weeks
1139	Deren	Whose
1140	Lokalisieren	Locate
1141	Mogen	To like
1142	Meinung	Opinion
1143	Charakter	Character
1144	Gekauft	Bought
1145	Insekt	Insect
1146	Dauernd	Constantly, continuously
1147	Gefangen	Caught
1148	Besonderes	Special
1149	Versucht	Tries, tried
1150	Zeigen	Indicate
1151	Funk	Radio
1152	Speiche	Spoke
1153	Stell	Put, *stell du vor* introduce yourself
1154	Sauer	Angry, *sauerteig* sourdough
1155	Perfekt	Perfect, complete, finished
1156	Wirkung	Effect
1157	Elektrisch	Electric
1158	Passt	Fits
1159	Erwarten	Expect
1160	Knochen	Bone
1161	Schiene	Rail
1162	Bieten	Provide
1163	Hoffentlich	Hopefully
1164	Hasse	Hate
1165	Zustimmen	Agree
1166	Sanft	Gentle
1167	Frei	Free
1168	Bekommt	Gets
1169	Kapitan	Captain
1170	Erraten	Guess
1171	Erforderlich	Necessary
1172	Witze	Jokes
1173	Scharf	Sharp

1174	Flugel	Wing
1175	Ungefahr	Approximately
1176	Schaffen	Create
1177	Nachbar	Neighbor
1178	Sowieso	Anyway
1179	Singt	Sings, *singt weiter* keep singing
1180	Wasch	Wash
1181	Fledermaus	Bat
1182	Eher	Rather
1183	Foto	Photograph
1184	Falls	If, in case, *wenn, ob, insofern*
1185	Mais	Corn
1186	Blod, blode	Stupid
1187	Vergleichen	Compare
1188	Ubrigens	By the way, incidentally
1189	Gedicht	Poem
1190	Schnur	String
1191	Glocke	Bell, clock
1192	Wasste	Desert
1193	Abhangen	Depend
1194	Fleisch	Meat
1195	Weh	Sore
1196	Einreiben	Rub
1197	Rohr	Tube
1198	Stolz	Proud, *stolz auf dich* proud of you
1199	Berahmt	Famous
1200	Schade	Too bad, *schadenfraude* malicious joy, *schaden* damage
1201	Mochten	Would like
1202	Strom	Stream, current
1203	Gratuliere	Congratulate
1204	Dagegen	On the other hand, against that,
1205	Dreieck	Triangle
1206	Band	Tape, strip, ribbon
1207	Eile	Hurry
1208	Chef	Chief
1209	Sitzt	Sits, *sitzt du?* Are you sitting?
1210	Kolonie	Colony
1211	Meines	Mine
1212	Liebling	Favorite
1213	Dinge	Things
1214	Krawatte	Tie
1215	Eingeben	Enter
1216	Krankenhaus	Hospital
1217	Dur	Major
1218	Krank	Ill, sick
1219	Frisch	Fresh
1220	Jedes	Each, *jedes mal* every time
1221	Suche	Search
1222	Senden	Send
1223	Gelb	Yellow
1224	Pistole	Gun

1225	Solche	Such
1226	Stiegen	Rose
1227	Erlauben	Allow
1228	Setz	Sit, *setz dich* sit down
1229	Druck	Print
1230	Scheint	Seems
1231	Nimmst	Take
1232	Stelle	Spot
1233	Anzug	Suit
1234	Liebt	Loves
1235	Klopfen	Beat, knocking
1236	Aufzug	Lift
1237	Gewinnen	Win
1238	Ankommen	Arrive
1239	Bescheid	Informed
1240	Stamm	Master
1241	Spur	Track
1242	Elternteil	Parent
1243	Wunderbar	Wonderful
1244	Ufer	Shore
1245	Wochenende	Weekend
1246	Teilung	Division
1247	Blatt	Sheet
1248	Spiele	Games
1249	Substanz	Substance
1250	Beganstigen	Favor
1251	Masste	Measured
1252	Hande	Hands
1253	Verbinden	Connect
1254	Hose	Trousers
1255	Getrennt	Cut, separated, disconnected
1256	Verbringen	Spend
1257	Akkord	Chord
1258	Behalten	To keep
1259	Fett	Fat
1260	Weile	While
1261	Wunschen	Want, wish, desire
1262	Wart	Wait
1263	Aktie	Share
1264	Nichte	Niece
1265	Tue	Do, *tue ich* I do
1266	Papa	Dad
1267	Traurig	Sad, sorry
1268	Brot	Bread
1269	Aufladen	Charge
1270	Nervos	Nervous
1271	Langsam	Slowly
1272	Leiste	Bar
1273	Angebot	Offer
1274	Kennt	Know, *kenntnis, kenntnisse* knowledge
1275	Kekse	Cookies

1276	Segelboot	Sailboat
1277	Karten	Cards, *karten spielen* playing cards
1278	Sklave	Slave
1279	Ente	Duck
1280	Jede	Each, any, every
1281	Markt	Market
1282	Fihlt	Feels
1283	Grad	Degree
1284	Besiedeln	Populate
1285	Fangen	To catch
1286	Kuken	Chick
1287	Euer	Your
1288	Ausgehen	Going out, also gehort
1289	Fiend	Enemy
1290	Alte	Old, olden, antique
1291	Antworten	Reply
1292	Getrink	Drink
1293	Auftreten	Occur
1294	Unseren	Ours
1295	Unterstatzung	Support
1296	Natur	Nature
1297	Total	Absolutely, totally
1298	Dampf	Steam
1299	Sagtest	Said, *sagtest du* you said, *sagtest du nicht* you did not say
1300	Bewegung	Motion
1301	Flussigkeit	Liquid
1302	Kaputt	Broken, *kaputt gehen* breaking down
1303	Protokollieren	Log
1304	Halt	Stop
1305	Toiletten	Restrooms
1306	Gebiss	Teeth
1307	Schale	Shell
1308	Hals	Neck
1309	Aussehen	Appearance
1310	Sauerstoff	Oxygen
1311	Ubel	Evil, see also *ungluck, unheil*
1312	Zucker	Sugar
1313	Wohnt	Lived, lives
1314	Weinen	To cry, weine nicht don't cry
1315	Geschicklichkeit	Skill
1316	Wein	Wine, *weintrauben* wine grapes
1317	Weihnachten	Christmas
1318	Saison	Season
1319	Losung	Solution
1320	Vorsichtig	Careful, *vorsichtig sein* be careful
1321	Silber	Silver
1322	Mies, miese	Lousy
1323	Magst	Like, *magst du* do you like?
1324	Zweig	Branch
1325	Langer	Longer, *langer weg* longer way

1327	Insbesondere	Especially
1328	Kuss	Kiss, *kuss zuruck* kiss back, *kussmund* kiss-mouth, pucker
1329	Feige	Fig
1330	Klingelt	Rings (noise), ringing
1331	Angstlich	Afraid
1332	Immerhin	After all
1333	Riesig	Huge
1334	Halte	Hold, hold on
1335	Grossmutter	Grandmother
1336	Stahl	Steel
1337	Diskutieren	Discuss
1338	Glaubt	Believes, trusts
1339	Vorwarts	Forward
1340	Ahnlich	Similar
1341	Wiegehts	How are you?
1342	Fragt	Asks
1343	Eigenartig	Strange
1344	Erfahrung	Experience
1345	Vagen	Vague
1346	Partitur	Score
1347	Apfel	Apple
1348	Bekomme	Get, obtain
1349	Gefahrt	Led
1350	Zieh	Pull, draw, attract
1351	Tonhahe	Pitch
1352	Zeug	Stuff, *zeuge* witness, *zeugenaussage* testimony
1353	Mantel	Coat
1354	Weise	Wise
1355	Masse	Mass
1356	Wahrheit	Truth
1357	Karte	Card
1358	Verdient	Earned
1359	Seil	Rope
1360	Rutsch	Slip
1361	Packen	To pack
1362	Masst	Measures
1363	Traumen	Dream
1364	Futtermittel	Feed
1365	Werkzeug	Tool
1366	Gesamt	Total
1367	Geruch	Smell
1368	Freue	Happy, *freue mich* I'm happy, *freuen* please, looking forward
1369	Tal	Valley
1370	Feiern	To celebrate
1371	Doppelt	Double
1372	Sitz	Seat
1373	Fortsetzen	Continue
1374	Bekommst	You get
1375	Versprochen	Promised
1376	Hut	Hat
1377	Verschwinden	Disappeared

1378	Verkaufen	Sell
1379	Verlieren	To lose
1380	Erfolg	Success
1381	Unten	Below, also *unteren*
1382	Firma	Company
1383	Tatsachlich	Actually, factually, really
1384	Spricht	Speaks
1385	Subtrahieren	Subtract
1386	Spinnst	Spinning, *spinnst du?* Are you spinning (are you crazy)?
1387	Veranstaltung	Event
1388	Schlimmer	Worse
1389	Schwimmen	Swim
1390	Begriff	Term
1391	Rief	Cried
1392	Gegenteil	Opposite
1393	Rauchen	Smoke, fumes
1394	Quatsch	Nonsense
1395	Prima	Great, *prima danke* great thanks
1396	Schuh	Shoe
1397	Onkel	Uncle
1398	Schulter	Shoulder
1399	Liegen	Lie, lying
1400	Verbreitung	Spread
1401	Arrangieren	Arrange
1402	Lager	Camp
1403	Leiden	Suffer
1404	Erfinden	Invent
1405	Baumwolle	Cotton
1406	Kuche	Kitchen, cusine, *kuchen* cake, *kuchen baken* bake a cake
1407	Geboren	Born
1408	Bestimmen	Determine
1409	Geredet	Talked
1410	Gefahrlich	Dangerous
1411	Genommen	Taken
1412	Neun	Nine
1413	Lastwagen	Truck
1414	Entschuldigt	Sorry
1415	Larm	Noise
1416	Arbeite	Work, labor
1417	Geschift	Shop
1418	Preiswertes	Inexpensive
1419	Wunsche	Wish
1420	Werfen	Throw
1421	Glanz	Shine
1422	Wofur	For what, for which, wherefore
1423	Immobilien	Property
1424	Willkommen	Welcome
1425	Spalte	Column
1426	Molekul	Molecule
1427	Richtigen	Correct, properly
1428	Pinkeln	PIN code

1429	Nachgedacht	Thoughts, reflection, pensees
1430	Grau	Gray
1431	Konntest	Could, can
1432	Wiederholung	Repeat
1433	Erfordern	Require
1434	Hierher	Here
1435	Gutes	Good
1436	Gekriegt	Got
1437	Merk	Notice, realize, pay attention to
1438	Vorbereiten	Prepare
1439	Salz	Salt
1440	Nase	Nose
1441	Namlich	Namely
1442	Mehreren	Plural
1443	Bezahlt	Paid
1444	Zorn	Anger
1445	Anspruch	Claim
1446	Anfang	Beginning
1447	Kontinent	Continent
1448	Womit	With which, wherewith
1449	Woruber	About which, whereof
1450	Wurdig	Worthy
1451	Kristal	Glass, crystal

Notes on German:

1. Once again, I have removed symbols related to pronunciation.

2. In General, an umlaut (OOM-Lot) (those two dots over a vowel) indicate that there are two vowels that should be pronounced separately. Köln, which is the city we would probably spell Cologne, can also be spelled Koeln. In this case, Köln is the same as Koeln and would be pronounced KO-EL-Nnnn (but more quickly than that, as if it were a single syllable, except that your tongue should move slightly between the O and the E, even if the E is only represented by an umlaut). Good luck with that. Just listen to the natives and do what they do; it'll all work out in the end. Also, that thing that looks like a large cursive B is actually SS.

3. Speaking of pronunciation: There's more than one form of German. In fact, each of the provinces (such as Bavaria, Westfalia, Schwabia, the Palatine, Etc.) has its own dialect and pronunciation. The common language that they all speak is called Hochdeutsch (High German). Nonetheless, Cologne has its own dialect, Kolnische; Berlin has Berlinische; Bavaria has Bayernische, etc. If you should visit Germany and hear something that sounds like German but doesn't match your phrase-book, you may be hearing a local dialect.

4. There are also different kinds of language for levels of formality. In the marketplace you may speak Hochdeustch among your friends; in the workplace you would speak Handelsdeutsch* among your coworkers, and the company executives would converse in AMT-Deutsch. It is my understanding – and my German-speaking friends have not been able to disabuse me of this notion, so I may err through sheer hard-headedness – that these strata are degrees of formality and accent, more than a separate dialect *per se*. For example, an English person might say "Innit?" (Isn't it?) among friends, but "Isn't that right?" in the office, and "Am I correct in believing so?" in a boardroom. Alternatively, an English person might speak with a Cockney or Liverpool accent among friends, but with RP (Received Pronunciation, or the BBC-World-Service accent) in a formal setting.

5. Speaking of accents: The tendency towards drawling seems to be most noticable in the North and West. In saying the word *Entschuldigen,* A Bayernische (Bavarian) might pronounce it very crisply, with clear enunciation, whereas a Kölnische might tend to slur it slightly. Towards the South of Germany, children are sometimes reprimanded to "Take the hot potato out of your mouth!" Apparently, this is one of many markers by which a German can identify the region and even the town from which other Germans come.

6. Given the above, there are some variant forms of various words. Also, like Serbo-Croat, there are many cases (but thankfully not as many as in Slavic languages, *Hvala Bogu!*). Most verbs can be ended in a –st form that is like the archaic English forms one sees in Shakespeare. *Gibe* (to give) may have a case *gibst* that might be read as the English "Giveth" or "Givest?" (Givest thou this unto me?). In fact, a good understanding of Jacobian English (the forms used by Shakespeare and the King James Translators) will go far towards helping with German grammar and sentence structure.

7. With all those factors, The "Thousand" words of German weighed in at 1451 words. You're welcome. Again, some of them are wrong.

8. Beware of "False Friends" or pseudo-cognates. One obvious example is "Gift" which means "Present" in English but "Poison" in German. "Nicht" looks like "Night" but it is "Not." "Lach" looks like "Lake" or "Loch" but it's "Laugh." *Kommen-sie Heir* sounds like "Come and see here" but actually just means "Come here." A friendly greeting of *Willkommen* (Welcome) sounds like a gruff "Well, come in." And so forth. One who is not aware of these false friend pseudo-cognates might easily mistake the speaker's intentions or attitude, especially in the last two examples. Be careful.

---

* Handelsdeutsch means "Trade German" or "Business German," and is not related to the composer, George Frederick Handel, best known for his opera, "Messiah."

FINNISH / SUOMI:

Polite phrases and Important ideas:

Please	Ole Kiltti (o-LAY KEEL-tee)
Thanks	Kiitos (KEE-toes)
Thank you	Kiitos (KEE-toes)
Thank you (emphasis)	Kiitos Paljon (KEE-toes Pal-YONE)
Excuse me (interrupting)	Anteeksi (ANT-EK-see)
Pardon me (for an error)	Anteeksi (ANT-EK-see)
Pardon me (for walking in front of someone)	Voi Anteeksi (VOY ANT-eksee)
Forgive me (for a grave error)	Anna Anteeksi (AHna ANT-eksee)
I'm sorry	Olen Paihoillani (OH len PAY-hoy-lonnie)
What is your name?	Mikä sinun nimesi on? (Mee-ka see-NOON nih-mee-see OHn?)
My name is…	Nimeni on … (Nih-MEE-nee On) ("I call myself…")
Where are the restrooms?	Missä ovat vessat? (Mee-sah oh-vat vess-shat?)

1	Yksi (OOksi)	6	Kuusi (KOOsee)	11	Yksitoista (OOKsee-TOY-stah)
2	Kaksi (KAHKsi)	7	Seitsemän (SETsee-man)	12	Kaksitoista (KAHKsee-toy-stah)
3	Kolme (KOHLme)	8	Kahdeksän (KAHKdeck-sand)	13	Kolmetoista
4	Neljä (NELLya)	9	Yhdeksän (OOdeck-sand)	14	Nelyahtoista
5	Viisi (VEEsee)	10	Kymmenen (COOmen-inn)	15	Viisitoista

16	Kuusitoista	21	Kaksikymmentayksi	70	Seitsemänkymmentä
17	Seitsemäntoista	30	Kolmekymmentä	80	Kahdeksänkymmentä
18	Kahdeksäntoista	40	Neljakymmentä	90	Yhdeksänkymmentä
19	Yhdeksäntoista	50	Viisikymmentä	100	Sata (SAH-TAH)
20	kaksikymmentä	60	Kuusikymmentä	1000	Tuhat (TOO-hot)

10,000 Kymmenentuhatta (COOmen-in-too-hot-tah)   1,000,000 Miljoona (MealYONE-uh)   0 Nolla (NOH-lah)

Odd Cases and Special Phrases:

Rakastan Sinua – *I love you.*	(Rrrock-es-stahn SEE-noo-ah)
Minä en tiedä, En tiedä – *I don't know, Dunno*	(Meenah-in-tee-AY-dah)(In-tee-AY-dah)
Ymmärrätkö?– *Do you understand?.*	(OOHmah-RAHT-kah)
Mutta kyllä / mutta ei - *But yes / but no*	(MooTAH KOOlah / MooTAH AIY)
Tule tänne – *Come here*	(TOO-lay TAHNnnnay)

In FINNISH, sentences may be formed as Subject-Verb-Object (*Minnen sinne,* I go there) but not Subject-Object-Verb. Subjects are usually blended with the verb, as with SPANISH. As in ENGLISH, noun modifiers are placed before the noun (*vihreä auto,* green car, not *auto vihreä,* green car).

1	kuin	as
2	olla	be, have
3	ja	and
4	minä	I
5	ei	no
6	hänen	his
7	että	that
8	se	it, that, this
9	hän	he
10	joka	which
11	oli	was
12	varten	for
13	päälle	on
14	myös	also
15	olemme	are
16	kanssa	with
17	saada	get
18	mutta	but
19	ne	they
20	tämä	this
21	klo	at
22	voida	can
23	tulla	become
24	yksi	one
25	Suomi	Finn, Finnish, Finland
26	tehdä	make, perform
27	alkaen	from
28	kun	when
29	mukaan	by
30	pitää	keep
31	kuuma	hot
32	sana	word
33	uusi	new
34	jo	already
35	mitä	what
36	hyvä	good, well, fine
37	jotkut	some
38	on	is
39	sanoa	say, tell, speak
40	kaikki	all, any, everything
41	sinua	you
42	markka	mark
43	tai	or
44	nyt	now
45	päälle	the
46	suuri	large, great
47	jos	of
48	kertoa	tell, multiply
49	tekeminen	making
50	vain	only, just
51	paljon	a lot, many much

52	muu	other, sundry
53	sisään	in
54	me	we
55	vielä	yet
56	niin	so, then
57	oma	own, personal, private
58	ulos	out
59	muut	other
60	sekä	mixed
61	mikä	what, that, which
62	olivat	were
63	maa	I, country, land
64	kaksi	two
65	niiden	their
66	aika	time
67	asia	thing, case, matter
68	tahtoa	will
69	he	they
70	miten	how
71	prosentti	percentage
72	sanoi	said
73	ihminen	man, person, human
74	pieni	an
75	kuitenkin	however, still, through
76	kukin	each
77	jälkeen	after, following
78	mies	man
79	tekee	does
80	setti	set
81	kolme	three
82	haluta	want
83	noin	about, approximately
84	hyvin	very, highly, very well
85	ilma	air
86	ensimmäinen	first, initial
87	jäädä	stay, remain
88	pelata	play
89	työ	work, job
90	ottaa	take, assume, receive
91	pää	end
92	antaa	give, deliver, submit
93	laittaa	put
94	koti	home
95	mieli	mind
96	lue	read
97	käsi	hand
98	alkaa	to start, to begin
99	portti	port
100	itse	self
101	oikeinkirjoituksen	spell
102	lisätä	add

103	moni	many, multi
104	jopa	even
105	käydä	visit
106	kaupunki	city
107	täällä	here
108	miljoona	million
109	must	must
110	iso	big
111	osa	part, portion, section
112	korkea	high
113	alue	area, range, zone
114	eikä	and not, neither
115	seurata	follow
116	säädös	act
117	miksi	why
118	päästä	to be released
119	kysyä	ask
120	vaikka	though
121	lapsi	child
122	miehet	men
123	muutos	change
124	päivä	day
125	hallitus	government, regime
126	meni	went
127	toimia	act, operate
128	valo	light
129	valmiiksi	ready
130	sama	same
131	koko	size
132	pois	off
133	tarvitsevat	need
134	ettei	lest
135	talo	house
136	kuva	picture
137	mennä	go
138	ensi	next, first, original
139	yrittää	try
140	kunta	municipality
141	meille	us
142	jälleen	again
143	toinen	second
144	eläin	animal
145	sillä	for
146	joutua	get, end up
147	kohta	point
148	äiti	mother
149	käyttää	use, exercise, wear
150	maailma	world
151	kuulua	belong, pertain
152	lähellä	near
153	mikään	any

154	rakentaa	build
155	nainen	woman
156	isä	father
157	viikko	week
158	esimerkiksi	for example
159	lähteä	start off, depart, go
160	eli	or
161	tarvita	need
162	yli	over
163	koska	because, since
164	paikka	place
165	Venäjä	Russia
166	tehty	made, done
167	Turku	Turkey
168	elää	live
169	luku	number
170	jossa	where
171	vanha	old
172	nousta	rise
173	pyöriä	rotate, roll, turn
174	nähdä	see, witness
175	takaisin	back
176	kerta	time
177	vähän	little
178	jokin	one
179	pyöreä	round
180	todeta	note
181	aikana	during
182	vuosi	year
183	yritys	company
184	tuli	came
185	nämä	these
186	tärkeä	important
187	alku	initial, beginning
188	minua	me
189	meidän	our
190	vaan	but
191	alle	under
192	tilanne	situation
193	nimi	name
194	presidentti	president
195	tieto	information
196	kautta	through
197	loppu	end, finish
198	amerikkalainen	American
199	lomake	form
200	onnettomuus	accident, misfortune
201	kallis	expensive
202	virke	sentence
203	uudistus	innovation, reform
204	ajatella	think

205	ase	gun
206	korvaus	compensation
207	auttaa	help
208	eteen	in front of, before
209	pelkästään	only, purely
210	alhainen	low
211	päätyä	end up
212	heikko	weak, fragile
213	mestaruus	championship, title
214	linja	line
215	erota	differ
216	säilyttää	retain
217	kyetä	be able to
218	vuoro	turn
219	syy	cause
220	ulkomainen	foreign
221	vastustaja	opponent, adversary
222	esiin	out, forward, bring forth
223	tarkoittaa	mean
224	ellei	unless
225	ennen	before
226	käräjäoikeus	district court
227	liikkua	move
228	eilen	yesterday
229	oikea	right
230	poika	boy
231	hieno	great
232	liian	too
233	työtön	thrust
234	siellä	there
235	kyseessä	at issue
236	kiertää	rotate, evade
237	ylös	up
238	Tukholma	Stockholm
239	sinun	your
240	taitaa	know
241	sotilas	soldier
242	tapa	way
243	tunnelma	atmosphere
244	aikainen	early
245	monet	many
246	pääkaupunki	capital
247	sitten	then
248	niitä	them
249	voimakas	strong, intense
250	kuvailla	portray, picture, narrate
251	kirjoittaa	write
252	kokonaisuus	whole, ensemble
253	olisi	would
254	kuten	like
255	tutustua	meet

256	tunnustaa	confess, acknowledge
257	venäläinen	Russian
258	viesti	message, relay
259	pitkä	long
260	ravintola	restaurant
261	ainoastaan	only, merely, just
262	Espanja	Spain
263	ehdottaa	propose, suggest, recommend
264	häntä	him
265	sallia	allow, permit, let
266	paljastaa	reveal, expose, uncover
267	kasvattaa	grow
268	katso	look
269	lisää	more
270	vero	tax
271	aamu	Morning
272	voisi	could
273	vuosittain	annually
274	kuolema	death, passing
275	tulevat	come
276	teki	did
277	pinta	surface
278	ääni	Sound
279	kadota	disappear
280	opiskella	study, train, learn
281	eniten	most
282	ihmiset	people
283	taito	skill, ability, knowledge
284	huomattavasti	considerably
285	minun	my
286	henkilökunta	staff, crew, brigade
287	tietää	know
288	nykyään	today
289	vesi	water
290	aiempi	prior
291	puhelu	call
292	puute	lack of
293	ohjaaja	supervisor
294	jotka	who
295	parhaillaan	presently
296	laatia	draw
297	saattaa	may
298	alas	down
299	tuolloin	then, at that time
300	juosta	run
301	puoli	half, side, aspect
302	ollut	been
303	vierailla	alongside
304	halpa	cheap, inexpensive
305	löytää	find
306	pari	pair

307	vaara	danger
308	seistä	stand
309	yksin	alone
310	sivu	page
311	pitäisi	should
312	poistaa	remove
313	löytyi	found
314	turha	useless
315	viranomainen	authoritative
316	vastaus	answer
317	esille	up, out
318	koulu	school
319	ikä	age, years
320	kasvaa	grow
321	maksu	payment
322	tutkimus	study
323	riski	risk
324	vielä	still, yet
325	oppia	learn
326	Tanska	Denmark
327	kasvi	plant
328	työnantaja	employer
329	kansi	cover
330	luovuttaa	alienate
331	ruoka	food
332	aurinko	sun
333	myönteinen	positive, favorable
334	tauti	disease, malady
335	joko	either
336	neljä	four
337	seutu	region, area
338	kylmä	cold
339	välillä	between
340	numero	number
341	valtio	state
342	vanhus	elder, senior citizen
343	liikaa	too much
344	aamulehti	Morning newspaper
345	järjestäjä	tracker
346	silmä	eye
347	ei koskaan	never
348	huippukokous	summit
349	eteenpäin	ahead, further on
350	viime	last
351	selkeä	clear
352	ajatus	thought
353	läpi	through
354	osapuoli	party
355	varsi	arm
356	puu	tree
357	kohtalo	destiny

358	samanlainen	similar, identical, same
359	astua	step, walk, tread
360	etelä, etelään	south
361	korjata	fix, repair
362	maatila	farm
363	kova	hard
364	painottaa	stress, emphasize, highlight
365	yhteisö	community
366	jatkossa	the future
367	ehkä	might
368	mielipide	opinion
369	taistella	fight, battle
370	tarina	story
371	Pohjola	North
372	saha	saw
373	pitkälle	far
374	kuunnella	listen
375	meri	sea
376	juhlia	celebrate, feast, party
377	piirtää	draw
378	Lontoo	London
379	vasen	left
380	samoin	likewise
381	keskimäärin	average
382	nenä	nose
383	eivät	don't
384	taata	guarantee
385	kuluttaja	consumer
386	taas	while
387	lehdistö	press
388	tuomio	judgment
389	erityisen, eritysesti	especially, particularly
390	lopullinen	final
391	yö	night
392	todellinen	real
393	väärä	wrong
394	elämä	life
395	kesken	in progress
396	harvat	few
397	laulaa	to sing
398	kunnanhallitus	municipal halls, municipal government
399	paperi	paper
400	toistaiseksi	for now
401	houkutella	to attract
402	pohjoiseen	north
403	tyhjä	blank, empty
404	kirja	book
405	lumi	snow
406	kuljettaa	carry
407	varsinainen	actual, ordinary
408	hotelli	hotel

409	yllätys	surprise
410	otti	took
411	ilo	joy, delight, pleasure
412	toimittaa	deliver, supply, provide
413	tiede	science
414	yltää	reach
415	kirjasto	library
416	viides	fifth
417	edessä	in front, ahead
418	harkita	consider, reflect
419	syödä	eat
420	huone	room
421	sinä	you
422	aikanaan	in due course, at the proper time
423	tekniikka	technique
424	homma	tomorrow
425	ystävä	friend
426	arvostella	criticise, review, judge
427	tähti	pace
428	alkoi	began
429	kulta	gold
430	harjoitella	carry on
431	kohdistua	focus
432	kala	fish
433	vaarallinen	dangerous
434	puhelin	phone
435	katsella	view
436	vuori	mountain
437	kehua	praise
438	lopettaa	stop
439	kerran	once
440	tasavalta	republic, commonwealth
441	tavoitella	pursue
442	huippu	peak
443	pohja	base
444	kuulla	hear
445	palauttaa	return
446	omistus	ownership, possession
447	hevonen	horse
448	valvonta	control, supervision
449	kysely	inquiry
450	viihtyä	prosper
451	leikkaus	cut
452	päättäjä	policy makers, decision makers
453	konserni	concern
454	vuorokausi	day
455	halu	desire, wish
456	varma	sure
457	hallinto	administration
458	orkesteri	orchestra
459	romaani	novel, Romany, Gypsy

460	väri	color
461	kasvot	face
462	uskaltaa	dare, venture
463	hankala	tricky, awkward
464	iltapäivä	afternoon
465	vienti	export
466	tärkein	main
467	teema	theme
468	helposti	easily
469	kannattaja	supporter, proponent
470	kiista	dispute
471	avoin	open
472	pörssi	stock market, exchange
473	allekirjoittaa	sign, endorse
474	kansallinen	national
475	näyttää	seem
476	ympäri	around, about
477	leiri	camp
478	lautakunta	board
479	yhdessä	together
480	seuraava	next
481	kannatus	support
482	suu	mouth
483	tuhota	destroy, ruin
484	tyytyä	settle for
485	rakenne	structure
486	valkoinen	white
487	lapset	children
488	varoittaa	warn, caution
489	tottua	get used to
490	sää	weather
491	kirjata	record, register, log
492	sai	got
493	arvella	believe, suppose, opine
494	kävellä	walk
495	puolustaa	defend
496	ministeriö	ministry
497	tausta	background
498	toukokuu	May
499	itsenäisyys	independency
500	helppous	ease
501	vedota	appeal
502	hyökkäys	attack, assault, offense
503	näky	sight
504	hehtaari	hectare
505	ruotsalainen	Swedish
506	vähetä	diminish
507	järvi	lake
508	Puola	Poland
509	ryhmä	group
510	harrastus	hobby, pursuit, interest

511	järjestäminen	organization
512	aina	always
513	helpottaa	facilitate
514	loma	holiday
515	opettaa	to teach, instruct
516	musiikki	music
517	Sveitsi	Switzerland
518	johtua	be due to
519	juna	train
520	tietenkin	of course, surely, doubtless
521	kaataa	pour
522	molemmat	both
523	sijoitus	investment
524	merkki	mark
525	pidättää	withhold, reserve
526	tilasto	statistics
527	sali	hall
528	usein	often
529	pistää	inject
530	asenne	stance
531	estää	prevent, stop, inhibit
532	kirje	letter
533	velka	debt
534	Lehtinen	flyer
535	maisema	landscape
536	saakka	until
537	vihreä	green
538	yliopisto	university
539	maili	mile
540	sanottu	called
541	aluksi	at first
542	joki	river
543	kuoro	choir
544	nimittäin	namely
545	auto	car
546	perustaminen	establishment, institution
547	lähde	source, spring
548	tarjous	offer, bid
549	jalat	feet
550	mielestä	with
551	sen	its
552	vika	fault
553	hoito	care
554	työvoima	labor, work force
555	lopulta	eventually, ultimately
556	Niemi	peninsula
557	vene	boat
558	todellisuus	reality
559	innostua	become inspired, find enthusiasm
560	tarpeeksi	enough
561	tavallinen	plain

562	pituus	length
563	tyttö	girl
564	rangaistus	penalty, sanction, punishment
565	nuori	young
566	pääkaupunkiseutu	metropolitan area
567	sekunti	second
568	helsinkiläinen	from Helsinki
569	valmis	ready
570	edellä	above
571	kuluessa	within
572	koskaan	ever
573	punainen	red
574	suoritus	performance, execution
575	lista	list
576	Unkari	Hungary
577	korva	ear, lug, flange
578	tässä	here
579	tuntea	feel
580	puhua	talk
581	yksilö	individual
582	kunnioittaa	respect, respected
583	lintu	bird
584	erillinen	separate, detached, distinct
585	pian	soon
586	elin	body
587	kunnes	until
588	koira	dog
589	lentokenttä	airport
590	perhe	family
591	säveltäjä	composer
592	suora	direct
593	aiheuttaa	pose
594	aikoina	in times of, in the era of
595	keskuspankki	central bank
596	erottaa	distinguish
597	jätä	leave
598	lupaus	promise
599	laulu	song
600	sektori	sector
601	Veikko	lad
602	aho	Meadow
603	mitata	measure
604	rehtori	principal
605	käynnistyä	start
606	sotilaallinen	military
607	mahdollisesti	possibly
608	ovi	door
609	vinkki	tip
610	opiskelu	study
611	urheilija	athlete
612	erityinen	special, specific, particular

613	tuote	product
614	kai	probably
615	kommentoida	comment, remark
616	dollari	dollar
617	kevyt	light
618	musta	black
619	yllättää	surprise
620	ammatti	profession, occupation, trade
621	hakemus	application, submission, petition
622	suhteen	regarding
623	väestö	population, folk
624	lyhyt	short
625	selkä	back
626	miljardi	billion
627	reitti	route
628	alueellinen	regional
629	edellyttää	require, demand, provide
630	järjestely	arrangement, scheme
631	milloin	when
632	paitsi	except
633	sitoa	tie, bind
634	suunnata	directed
635	haitata	hinder, impede, inhibit
636	poiketa	diverge, digress
637	ammattilainen	professional
638	luokka	class
639	usko	belief
640	kulutus	consumption
641	melkoinen	sizable
642	hyväksi	for, on behalf of, for the benefit of
643	tuuli	wind
644	hiihto	skiing
645	kauppias	dealer
646	kysymys	question
647	talli	stable, barn
648	edistää	promote, encourage, foster
649	keskuudessa	among, amongst
650	hiukan	a little
651	posti	postal
652	siten	so
653	tapahtua	happen
654	täydellinen	complete
655	tuomari	judge
656	ilmoitus	notice, notification, message
657	nousu	increase
658	vanki	prisoner, captive
659	ilmiö	phenomenon
660	laiva	ship
661	ranskalainen	French
662	sairaus	disease
663	suorastaan	downright

664	neljäs	fourth
665	työelämä	working life
666	teho	power
667	oikeudenkäynti	litigation, trial
668	tapauksessa	event
669	tarttua	stick
670	herra	Sir
671	päästää	let, allow, release, emit
672	kallio	rock
673	rivi	line
674	järjestys	order
675	mennessä	by
676	taho	quarter
677	surmata	slay, destroy
678	valtava	huge, vast
679	kiinnostus	interest
680	itsenäinen	independent
681	palo	fire
682	hyödyntää	utilize, make use of, exploit
683	neuvosto	council
684	arkisto	archive, records, files
685	moottori	engine
686	eduskuntaryhmä	parliamentary group
687	verrata	compare
688	ohje	guide
689	ongelma	problem
690	asettua	settle, moderate, settle down
691	pala	piece
692	tähän	over here
693	toimisto	office
694	henkilöauto	passenger car
695	matkustaa	travel
696	kertoi	told
697	levitä	extend, spread
698	kyky	ability, capacity
699	takainen	behind
700	keskelläin	the middle
701	tiesi	knew
702	kolmannes	a third of
703	kulkea	pass
704	pelastaa	to save
705	kustannus	publishing
706	porukka	group, outfit, company, companions
707	etukäteen	in advance, up front
708	alkuun	top
709	johtava	leading
710	osallistuminen	involvement
711	pääosa	bulk, main body, largest part
712	paikalla	present (i.e. at the place)
713	myötä	with
714	runo	poem

715	vamma	injury
716	kuningas	king
717	vähä	wax
718	ohi	past
719	Pariisi	Paris
720	toimittaja	supplier, provider
721	katu	street
722	työllisyys	employment
723	alkuperäinen	original, primary, indigenous
724	tosiasia	fact
725	ruumis	corpse
726	lukija	reader
727	tuuma	inch
728	lisääntyä	multiply
729	tasainen	flat
730	arvoinen	worth
731	ei mitään	nothing
732	silloin	then, at the time
733	haitta	disadvantage
734	kurssi	course
735	ostaja	buyer
736	pysyä	stay
737	luonne	temperament, character, nature
738	pyörä	wheel
739	elintarvike	grocery, foods
740	täysi	full
741	eläkeläinen	retiree
742	voima	force, power
743	sininen	blue
744	esine	object
745	jäljellä	left
746	maalata	paint, spray
747	päättää	decide
748	ehdoton	absolute, unconditional, categorical
749	syvä	deep
750	saari	island
751	uudistaa	renew, reform
752	jalka	foot
753	vähentyä	decrease
754	erä	batch, round, installment
755	järjestelmä	system
756	väite	claim
757	kiireinen	busy
758	päivittäin	daily
759	testi	test
760	ennätys	record
761	toiminto	function
762	Kirsi	soil frost
763	veneen	boat
764	ajankohta	timing
765	yhteinen	common

766	aikaisin	early, beforetimes
767	Viro	Estonia
768	prosessi	process, proceedings
769	mahdollinen	possible
770	serbi	Serb
771	tavoittaa	reach, catch
772	kone	plane
773	Laine	wave
774	sijaansa	stead
775	valtioneuvosto	council of state
776	kuiva	dry
777	palvelus	service, favor
778	parantaa	improve
779	ihme	wonder
780	rahasto	fund, trust, treasury
781	kissa	cat
782	nauraa	laugh
783	tuhatta	thousand
784	Arja	Aryan
785	maaliskuu	March
786	päällikkö	chief
787	sentti	cent, centimeter
788	demokratia	democracy
789	juoksi	ran
790	sentään	at least
791	soittaa	call
792	kirjoitus	writing, script
793	laajentaa	expand
794	tarkistaa	check
795	hävitä	lose, disappear, wear off
796	palaa	burn, ignite
797	peli	game
798	mahdoton	impossible, unthinkable
799	muoto	shape
800	avustus	aid, allowance
801	rinnastaa	equate
802	Hollanti	Dutch
803	kouluttaa	pains
804	kaikkea	all
805	neiti	miss
806	paeta	escape
807	selvitä	clarify
808	surma	death
809	tori	market
810	tuomita	condemn
811	nimetä	name
812	odotus	waiting
813	toi	brought
814	lämpö	heat
815	julistaa	declare
816	rengas	ring

817	mukainen	adequate
818	tuoda	bring
819	kyllä	yes
820	Kokoomus	coalition
821	sosiaalinen	social
822	kaukainen	distant
823	museo	museum
824	maailmancup	world
825	lopputulos	result
826	täyttää	fill
827	ennustaa	forecast
828	itään	east
829	äänestys	Voting, polling, ballot
830	kohdalla	under
831	maali	paint
832	kieli	language
833	sattua	occur
834	todistaa	prove
835	käsitys	understanding, idea
836	näkökulma	perspective
837	ansiosta	thanks
838	luulla	think, believe, suppose
839	yksikkö	unit
840	lainkaan	at all, any
841	ylimääräinen	extra, spare
842	hyöty	benefit, advantage, profit
843	urheilu	sport
844	taakse	behind
845	seinä	wall
846	kuvitella	imagine
847	osoittautua	prove
848	tietty	certain
849	huume	drug
850	kiinnostaa	interest
851	muualla	elsewhere
852	lentää	fly
853	vähäinen	low, waxen
854	pelko	fear, dread
855	pudota	fall
856	verran	about
857	johtaa	lead
858	itkeä	cry
859	sähkö	electric
860	uusia	renew
861	vierailu	stay
862	muodostua	form
863	pimeä	dark
864	työllistää	employ
865	huomautus	note
866	investointi	investment
867	liki	almost

868	pöytä	table
869	Kesk	among
870	odottaa	wait
871	turnaus	tournament
872	uhata	threaten, menace
873	purkaa	land
874	suunnitelma	plan
875	tietokone	computer
876	maatalous	agricultural
877	puolustus	defense
878	uhka	threat
879	laatikko	box
880	saaminen	claim
881	aine	substance, material, matter
882	tappaa	kill, murder
883	substantiivi	noun
884	yhtään	any
885	Itävalta	Austria
886	keksiä	invent
887	kenttä	field
888	levätä	rest
889	toive	wish, desire
890	valmistautua	get ready, prepare, make preparations
891	kakkonen	two, deuce
892	pelätä	to be afraid
893	puolesta	on behalf of
894	täynnä	full, filled
895	tuotto	yield, profit
896	lakko	strike, walkout
897	sisältyä	include
898	kohti	towards
899	pystyy	able
900	tapaaminen	meeting
901	punta	pound
902	sosiaali-	social
903	paikkakunta	location, destination
904	kehottaa	urge
905	kauneus	beauty
906	ajaa	drive
907	korko	interest
908	lähestyä	approach, draw near
909	puhe	speech, speaking
910	seisoi	stood
911	paluu	return
912	Vesa	sprout
913	sukupolvi	generation
914	tuottaja	producer, showman
915	ulkopuolella	outside
916	sisältävät	contain
917	etuosa	front
918	kiinteistö	property

919	auki	open, loose, unlocked
920	henkinen	spiritual
921	pakottaa	force, compel, oblige
922	päiväkoti	nursery
923	antoi	gave
924	ennakoida	anticipate
925	luottaa	trust
926	nykyisin	nowadays
927	palkata	hire, retain
928	verotus	taxation
929	ansaita	earn, gain, win
930	kaupunginjohtaja	mayor
931	kohtaan	towards
932	politiikka	policy, politics
933	oi	oh
934	nopea	quick
935	maalaus	painting
936	kehittää	develop
937	alus	ship, vessel, craft
938	marraskuu	November
939	sitoutua	commit
940	selvitys	statement, account
941	valtameri	ocean
942	isäntä	host, landlord
943	tonni	ton
944	iloinen	cheerful, happy, glad
945	kiire	hurry, rush, urgency
946	lämmin	warm
947	ilmetä	manifest itself, appear, come into sight
948	nimenomaan	specifically
949	ikkuna	window
950	kiittää	thank, command
951	vapaa	free
952	huonosti	badly
953	minuutti	minute
954	bändi	band
955	huoli	worry
956	kortti	card
957	vara	spare
958	aktiivinen	active
959	vahva	strong
960	erityistä	special
961	kiitos	thank you
962	jääkiekko	hockey
963	kaikkein	very, much
964	loistaa	shine
965	omistaa	possess, own, hold (property)
966	ralli	rally
967	suosikki	favorite
968	tosi	true
969	tuo	that

970	turvata	secure
971	takana	behind
972	pyrstö	tail
973	tuottaa	produce
974	oikeastaan	really
975	voimakkaasti	strongly
976	pahasti	badly
977	tiukka	tight, strict
978	lento	flight
979	tilaa	space
980	kuuli	heard
981	luonto	nature, wildlife
982	luonnehtia	define
983	paras	best
984	tunti	hour
985	parempi	better
986	jonkin	something
987	osittain	partly
988	totta	True
989	Ynnol	copyright
990	sata	hundred
991	viisi	five
992	muistaa	remember
993	vaihe	step
994	jäsenyys	membership
995	julkinen	public
996	varhainen	early
997	pidä	hold
998	yhdistää	compound
999	länsi	west
1000	kääntää	turn, flip, translate
1001	korotus	raise
1002	etua	interest
1003	parata	improve
1004	perustella	justify
1005	nopeasti	fast
1006	verbi	verb
1007	kauan	long
1008	kutsua	invite
1009	kierros	round
1010	kuusi	six
1011	panna	put
1012	tarkasti	closely
1013	elokuu	August
1014	joskus	sometimes
1015	riittävästi	sufficiently
1016	tänne	here
1017	taulukko	table
1018	matkailu	travel
1019	vähemmän	less
1020	Vas	left

1021	joulukuu	December
1022	kymmenen	ten
1023	kesäkuu	June
1024	kokonaan	wholly, fully
1025	mikäli	provided
1026	pääsy	access
1027	taiteilija	artist
1028	edetä	proceed, advance
1029	heinäkuu	July
1030	keskittyä	centralize
1031	parantaminen	betterment, improvement
1032	yksinkertainen	simple
1033	useat	several
1034	Itä-Timor	East Timor
1035	kaltainen	like, similar, akin
1036	kantaa	carry
1037	vokaali	vowel
1038	sota	war
1039	asettaa	lay
1040	lähtökohta	starting point
1041	maku	taste
1042	vastaan	against
1043	kuvio	pattern
1044	edellytys	prerequisite
1045	hidas	slow
1046	lukuunottamatta	except for
1047	kanava	channel, duct, canal
1048	keskus	center
1049	rakkaus	love
1050	henkilö	person
1051	lääkäri	doctor
1052	kysellä	ask
1053	lukuisa	numerous
1054	onni	luck
1055	käynnistää	kick off
1056	raha	money
1057	palvella	serve
1058	valtuusto	council
1059	ilmestyä	appear
1060	tie	road
1061	kartta	map
1062	sija	position, place, spot
1063	suoraan	straight, directly
1064	öljy	oil
1065	liiga	league
1066	sade	rain
1067	kilpailija	rival, competitor
1068	sääntö	rule
1069	valta	power
1070	varsinkin	especially
1071	kaikkiaan	in all, all told

1072	säätelevät	govern
1073	varmaan	will
1074	yhdistys	association
1075	arvokas	valuable
1076	kampanja	campaign, crusade
1077	valmistaa	prepare, manufacture, produce
1078	vetää	pull
1079	kohota	rise
1080	omistaja	owner, possessor
1081	pärjätä	to manage
1082	tulkinta	interpretation
1083	tuore	fresh
1084	komea	handsome, magnificent
1085	liikunta	exercise, workout
1086	matkustaja	passenger
1087	periä	charge, collect
1088	periaate	principle
1089	energia	energy
1090	hopea	silver
1091	metsästää	hunt
1092	todennäköinen	probable
1093	huomauttaa	points out, indicates
1094	sängyssä	bed
1095	kieltää	prohibit
1096	haastattelu	interview
1097	perustua	base on, use as a basis for
1098	veli	brother
1099	osaaminen	know-how, skill, ability
1100	muna	egg
1101	ratsastaa	ride
1102	solu	cell
1103	oppositio	opposition
1104	uskoa	believe
1105	oppilas	pupil, student, disciple
1106	harrastaa	cultivate
1107	poimia	pick
1108	äkillinen	sudden
1109	neliö	square
1110	harjoitus	training, drill, exercise
1111	edustaa	represent
1112	keino	means, ways
1113	pohjoinen	North
1114	taide	art
1115	aihe	subject
1116	kotimainen	domestic
1117	hallinta	possession, mastery, occupation of
1118	uudelleen	again
1119	vaihdella	vary
1120	paino	weight
1121	tehdas	factory
1122	yleinen	general

1123	jää	ice
1124	ympyrä	circle
1125	kahtiajaon	divide
1126	kiekko	puck
1127	tavu	syllable
1128	huopa	felt
1129	pallo	ball
1130	aalto	Wave
1131	Lappi	Lapland
1132	ajan	I drive
1133	saavuttaa	reach
1134	sydän	heart
1135	sijoittaa	place, accommodate
1136	tilaisuus	opportunity
1137	nykyinen	present
1138	olo	feeling
1139	tammikuu	January
1140	raskas	heavy
1141	palkinto	prize, reward
1142	virka	post
1143	konsertti	concert
1144	tanssi	dance
1145	rauha	peace
1146	katsoja	viewer
1147	pelkkä	mere, block
1148	asema	position
1149	pakolainen	refugee
1150	kriisi	crisis
1151	ulkomaa	abroad
1152	keskeinen	key
1153	leveä	wide
1154	palkka	pay
1155	kehittäminen	generation, cultivation
1156	Keski-Suomi	middle-Finland
1157	katto	roof
1158	mainita	mention, quote
1159	juhla	celebration, feast, festival
1160	purje	sail
1161	koostua	consist of
1162	levy	plate, disc
1163	lokakuu	October
1164	luottamus	confidence
1165	materiaali	material
1166	menettää	lose
1167	tilata	order
1168	perusteella	by
1169	piiri	circuit, district
1170	vajaa	short
1171	harva	few, thin, sparse
1172	lippu	ticket
1173	syyskuu	September

1174	toimi	action
1175	historiallinen	historical
1176	julkisuus	publicity
1177	keskustella	debate, talk
1178	maajoukkue	national team
1179	metsä	forest
1180	rajoittaa	restrict, limit
1181	yhtye	band, group
1182	sulkea	close, exclude
1183	vaihtua	change, switch
1184	istua	sit
1185	määrätä	determine
1186	yksittäinen	single, isolated
1187	harvinainen	rare, uncommon, infrequent
1188	teko	artificial
1189	turva	safety
1190	määritellä	the amounts
1191	satama	port
1192	enemmistö	majority, preponderance
1193	kilpailu	race
1194	lasku	fall, invoice, landing
1195	teatteri	theatre
1196	sisältö	contents
1197	hauska, hauskaa	fun, amusing
1198	leikata	cut, trim, excise
1199	puolitoista	one and a half
1200	taivas	sky
1201	halli	hall, passage
1202	myymälä	store
1203	vaihde	gear
1204	valtaosa	the greater part
1205	kesä	summer
1206	lääke	medicine, drug
1207	kelvata	do
1208	laina	a loan
1209	uni	sleep
1210	väkivalta	violence
1211	silta	bridge
1212	hylätä	to reject
1213	paikalle	the scene, the location
1214	yhteydessä	in connection with
1215	aste	degree, grade
1216	yksinäinen	lone
1217	juuri	just, right
1218	suunnittelu	design, planning
1219	vaihtaa	change, exchange
1220	syyte	charge, indictment
1221	maalivahti	keeper, goalie
1222	vähentää	subtract
1223	koota	assemble
1224	saalis	catch

1225	toivottaa	wish
1226	lauta	board
1227	talvi	winter
1228	kyll	sat
1229	kirjallinen	written
1230	villi	wild
1231	väline	instrument
1232	säilytettävä	kept
1233	lasi	glass
1234	ruoho	grass
1235	lehmä	cow
1236	reuna	edge
1237	Vierailun	visit
1238	pehmeä	soft
1239	kirkas	bright
1240	kaasu	gas
1241	kuukausi	month
1242	viimeistely	finish
1243	onnellinen	happy
1244	Toivottavasti	hope
1245	kukka	flower
1246	pitkin	along
1247	vaatettaa	clothe
1248	outo	strange
1249	poissa	gone
1250	kauppa	trade
1251	käyttäjä	user
1252	kiistää	contest, dispute
1253	karhu	bear
1254	tähdätä	target
1255	melodia	melody
1256	matka	trip
1257	vastaanottaa	receive
1258	Halonen	one hall
1259	poistua	exit, retire
1260	kirjallisuus	literature
1261	kyse	about
1262	väki	people
1263	tarkka	exact
1264	vieras	guest
1265	kaivata	miss, need, yearn
1266	rikkoa	break, violate
1267	symboli	symbol
1268	potilas	patient, case (medical)
1269	vähiten	least
1270	alla	below
1271	ongelmia	trouble
1272	huutaa	shout
1273	kulttuuri	culture, cultivation
1274	äänestää	Vote
1275	kirjoitti	wrote

1276	budjetti	budget
1277	siemen	seed
1278	laitos	institute
1279	sävy	tone
1280	varata	book
1281	yhtyä	join
1282	lyödä	knock, hit, beat
1283	puhtaita	clean
1284	sijoittua	get a place
1285	tauko	break
1286	näytelmä	play
1287	piha	yard
1288	menestys	success
1289	arvio	estimate, evaluation
1290	huono	bad
1291	puhallus	blow
1292	rata	track, course
1293	kirjailija	author
1294	saksalainen	German
1295	veri	blood
1296	voittaja	winner, victor
1297	kappale	paragraph
1298	koskettaa	touch
1299	kasvoi	grew
1300	turvallisuus	safety
1301	sekoittaa	mix
1302	joukkue	team
1303	lähtö	departure
1304	lanka	wire
1305	ainakaan	at least not, certainly not
1306	kustannukset	cost
1307	menetetty	lost
1308	ranta	sleet, beach, shore
1309	ruskea	brown
1310	kuluminen	wear
1311	luopua	abandon, resign
1312	puutarha	garden
1313	ulkoministeri	foreign ministry
1314	yhtäläinen	equal
1315	heittää	throw, cast, toss
1316	lähetetty	sent
1317	valita	choose, Select
1318	laski	fell
1319	sovittaa	fit
1320	virtaus	flow
1321	oikeudenmukainen	fair
1322	pankki	bank
1323	kerätä	collect
1324	tallentaa	save
1325	ohjaus	control
1326	desimaalin	decimal

1327	melko	quite
1328	rikkoi	broke
1329	hetki	moment
1330	asteikko	scale
1331	äänekäs	Loud
1332	kevät	spring
1333	tarkkailla	observe
1334	konsonantti	consonant
1335	kansakunta	nation
1336	sanakirja	dictionary
1337	maito	milk
1338	nopeus	speed
1339	menetelmä	method
1340	säästää	save
1341	ura	career
1342	urut	organ
1343	väliin	between
1344	yrittäjä	entrepreneur
1345	maksaa	pay
1346	jakso	section
1347	mekko	dress
1348	pilvi	cloud
1349	hiljainen	quiet
1350	kivi	stone
1351	pikkuruinen	tiny
1352	kiivetä	climb
1353	viileä	cool
1354	kehno	poor
1355	kokeilu	experiment
1356	avain	key
1357	rauta	iron
1358	tietysti	naturally, needless to say
1359	kaksikymmentä	twenty
1360	iho	skin
1361	hymy	smile
1362	prässi	crease
1363	reikä	hole
1364	hyppy	jump
1365	vauva	baby
1366	kahdeksan	eight
1367	kylä	village
1368	tavata	meet
1369	ostaa	buy
1370	nostaa	raise
1371	ratkaista	solve
1372	metalli	metal
1373	onko	whether
1374	alkuvuosi	early
1375	seitsemän	seven
1376	kolmas	third

1378	hiukset	hair
1379	kuvata	describe
1380	kokki	cook
1381	lattia	floor
1382	jompikumpi	either
1383	tulos	result
1384	polttaa	burn
1385	mäki	hill
1386	turvallinen	safe
1387	luvulla	century
1388	tyyppi	type
1389	laki	law
1390	bitti	bit
1391	rannikolla	coast
1392	kopio	copy
1393	lause	phrase
1394	pitkä	tall
1395	hiekka	sand
1396	maaperä	soil
1397	rulla	roll
1398	lämpötila	temperature
1399	sormi	finger
1400	teollisuus	industry
1401	arvo	value
1402	taistelu	fight
1403	valhe	lie
1404	voittaa	beat, win, overcome
1405	kiihottaa	excite
1406	luonnollinen	natural
1407	välttää	avoid
1408	näkymä	view
1409	merkityksessä	sense
1410	pääoma	capital
1411	tuoli	chair
1412	hedelmät	fruit
1413	rikas	rich
1414	paksu	thick
1415	toimivat	operate
1416	käytäntö	practice
1417	vaikea	difficult
1418	olkaa hyvä	please
1419	suojella	protect
1420	keskipäivällä	noon
1421	kasvuston	crop
1422	nykyaikainen	modern
1423	elementti	element
1424	osuma	hit
1425	opiskelija	student
1426	kulma	corner
1427	lama	recession, economic slump
1428	vaate	garment

1429	aloite	initiative
1430	puolue	party
1431	yhteiskunnallinen	social
1432	tarjonta	supply
1433	joiden	whose
1434	paikantaa	locate
1435	hyönteinen	insect
1436	kiinni	caught
1437	osoittaa	indicate
1438	puhui	spoke
1439	atomi	atom
1440	ihmisen	human
1441	historia	history
1442	vaikutus	effect
1443	sähköinen	electric
1444	luu	bone
1445	kisko	rail
1446	suostua	agree
1447	näin	thus
1448	lempeä	gentle
1449	kapteeni	captain
1450	arvata	guess
1451	välttämätön	necessary
1452	teräviä	sharp
1453	siipi	wing
1454	luoda	create
1455	naapuri	neighbor
1456	pesu	wash
1457	lepakko	bat
1458	pikemminkin	rather
1459	väkijoukko	crowd
1460	maissi	corn
1461	vertaa	compare
1462	soittokello	bell
1463	riippua	depend
1464	liha	meat
1465	hieroa	rub
1466	putki	tube
1467	kuuluisa	famous
1468	virta	stream
1469	ohut	thin
1470	kolmio	triangle
1471	planeetta	planet
1472	siirtomaa	colony
1473	kello	clock
1474	merkittävä	major
1475	haku	search
1476	lähettää	send
1477	keltainen	yellow
1478	painatus	print
1479	kuollut	dead

1480	aavikko	Desert
1481	puku	suit
1482	hissi	lift
1483	saapua	arrive
1484	mestari	master
1485	raita	track
1486	vanhempi	parent
1487	rannikko	shore
1488	jako	division
1489	arkki	sheet
1490	suosia	favor
1491	kytkeä	connect
1492	viettää	spend
1493	sointu	chord
1494	rasva	fat
1495	osake	share
1496	isä	dad
1497	leipä	bread
1498	veloittaa	charge
1499	segmentti	segment
1500	orja	slave
1501	säästö	savings
1502	ankka	duck
1503	valinta	selection, option
1504	välitön	instant
1505	markkinat	market
1506	asuttaa	populate
1507	poikasen	chick
1508	rakas	dear
1509	vihollinen	enemy
1510	vastata	reply
1511	juoma	drink
1512	esiintyä	occur
1513	tuki	support
1514	höyry	steam
1515	polku	path
1516	neste	liquid
1517	loki	log
1518	tarkoitti	meant
1519	osamäärä	quotient
1520	hampaat	teeth
1521	kuori	shell
1522	niska	neck
1523	happi	oxygen
1524	sokeri	sugar
1525	naiset	women
1526	kausi	season
1527	ratkaisu	solution
1528	magneetti	magnet
1529	sivuliike	branch
1530	ottelu	match

1531	pääte	suffix
1532	viikuna	fig
1533	peloissaan	afraid
1534	sisko	sister
1535	teräs	steel
1536	samankaltainen	similar
1537	opas	guide
1538	kokemus	experience
1539	pisteet	score
1540	omena	apple
1541	ostivat	bought
1542	led	led
1543	piki	pitch
1544	takki	coat
1545	massa	mass
1546	köysi	rope
1547	lipsahdus	slip
1548	unelma	dream
1549	ilta	evening
1550	ehto	condition
1551	rehu	feed
1552	työkalu	tool
1553	yhteensä	total
1554	perus	basic
1555	haju	smell
1556	laakso	valley
1557	eikä myöskään	nor
1558	kaksinkertainen	double
1559	istuin	seat
1560	jatkaa	continue
1561	lohko	block
1562	kaavio	chart
1563	ympäristö	surroundings
1564	hattu	hat
1565	myydä	sell
1566	tapahtuma	event
1567	sopimus	deal
1568	uida	swim
1569	termi	term
1570	päinvastainen	opposite
1571	vaimo	wife
1572	kenkä	shoe
1573	olkapää	shoulder
1574	leviäminen	spread
1575	muisto	memory, remembrance
1576	puuvilla	cotton
1577	määrittää	determine
1578	sairaala	hospital
1579	välittää	convey
1580	yhdeksän	nine
1581	melu	noise

1582	taso	level
1583	mahdollisuus	chance
1584	venyttää	stretch
1585	paistaa	shine
1586	omaisuus	property
1587	sarake	column
1588	molekyyli	molecule
1589	harmaa	gray
1590	toistaa	repeat
1591	vaatia	require
1592	laaja	broad
1593	valmistella	prepare
1594	suola	salt
1595	monikko	plural
1596	viha	anger
1597	vaatimus	claim
1598	ministeri	minister
1599	vahvasti	confirmed
1600	terveys	health
1601	rahoittaa	finance
1602	alkoholi	Alcohol
1603	projekti	Project

Notes on Finnish:

1. There's an old joke – I first read it in *How to Learn Any Langauge*, Barry M. Farber, but it probably predates that book – about how Finnish is related to Hungarian, but the Finns got all the vowels. It is true that Finnish has many more vowels than any language fairly needs, but in this it seems to me to have some kinship to Estonian. But even the Estonian versions of the same words seem to have fewer vowels than Finnish (Kolm, Kolme). I am going to make a wild, hairy assumption here, based entirely on ignorance, that the differences between Finnish and Hungarian come from their environments. Finnish has adapted to its Baltic environment, and thus shows a certain kinship to Estonian and Lithuanuan; Hungarian has adapted to its Central European environment, and thus shows a certain kinship to Slavic languages. This resolves the paradox of two related tongues, one heavy in vowels, and one virtually breft of vowels.

2. I also note that the number of vowels could cause a casual observer to compare it with Samoan or Hawaiian, even though there is not and cannot be any relationship whatsoever.

3. Like German, it is possible to compound words to make new words. As an example, note the word kaksikymmentätuhatta (twenty thousand). It literally reads "Two ten thousand," and makes a single word of them.

4. An advantage of Finnish is that there appear to be very few cognates and borrow words. This keeps us from being distracted by false friends, and from being tempted to rely on familiar forms.

5. Finnish has a number of cases, but these appear to be much more manageable than in Slavic languages. I have not been able to distinguish all of the cases, but it's not the point of this book to teach grammar. This book is a vocabulary only.

Index:

T

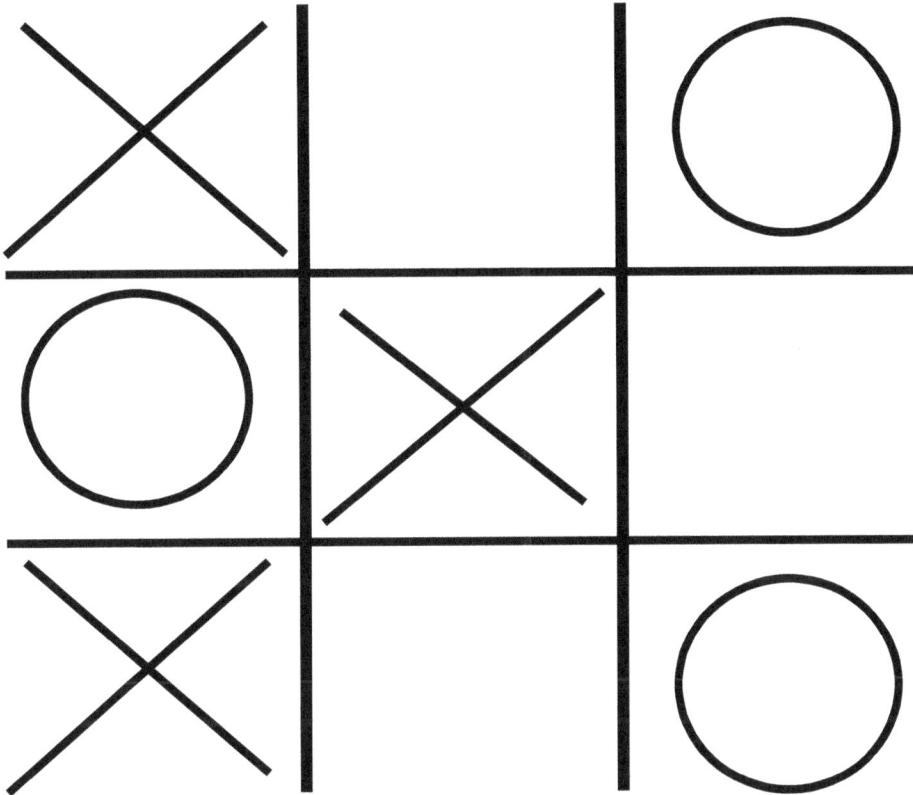

www.ingramcontent.com/pod-product-compliance
Lightning Source LLC
Chambersburg PA
CBHW080555090426

42735CB00016B/3240